ONE DAY BETTER

ONE DAY BETTER

Mental Performance Concepts to Transform Your Game and Life

JEFF TROESCH

PUBLISHING

80/20 Publishing, LLC
1073 Oberland Drive
Midway, UT 84043
www.8020books.com

Library of Congress Control Number: 2025939791
ISBN 979-8-9907958-4-6 print
ISBN 979-8-9907958-5-3 ebook

Cover and interior design by Vicki Hopewell
Author photo courtesy of the author

For the countless thousands of athletes, coaches,
and other people in all walks of life who have blessed me
with the opportunity to learn from them, to grow with them,
and to support their journeys toward excellence and mastery.

For those who read this book and have
some small seed planted that might be cultivated
into something fruitful and useful in their lives.

My fervent desire is that after I am gone this book might
live on as a continuation of the intention of my life's work,
which is to help people live more productive,
peaceful, and fulfilled lives.

CONTENTS

Foreword . . . x
Preface . . . xiii
Introduction . . . xvii

1 One Day Better . . . 1
2 Commit to Mastery . . . 4
3 Effective vs. Right . . . 7
4 Mental Discipline Matters More Than Toughness . . . 9
5 Response Ability . . . 12
6 Trust vs. Commitment . . . 14
7 Be a Scientist, Not a Judge . . . 16
8 Awareness vs. Attention . . . 18
9 Have a Purpose in Mind . . . 20
10 Focus on What to Do, Not What It Means . . . 22
11 Belief, Decisiveness, and Commitment . . . 24
12 Be Here Now . . . 26
13 Develop Routines and Rituals . . . 28
14 You Can't Steal Second with One Foot on First . . . 31
15 Breathe . . . 33
16 Do You Hit the Gas Pedal or the Brakes? . . . 35
17 Approach or Avoid? . . . 37
18 Look at the Target . . . or Don't . . . 39
19 Increase the Odds . . . 41
20 ACE: Score the Controllables . . . 43
21 Every Rep Matters . . . 45
22 What Will You Do Next Time? . . . 46
23 Eliminate the Shoulds, Needs, and Have-Tos . . . 48
24 Build a Callus . . . 50
25 What Triggers Your Attentional Drift? . . . 52
26 Current Events, Not History . . . 54
27 Incorporate Recovery into Your Routine . . . 55
28 What If They Called You a Chair? . . . 57
29 Think About an Elephant . . . 59
30 Accept Your Role . . . 61
31 How Do You Affect Your Environment? . . . 63
32 Make Sure the Last Thing You Do Is Positive . . . 65
33 Honestly and Accurately Evaluate Yourself . . . 67

34 Acceptance vs. Satisfaction 69
35 Reaction vs. Response 70
36 Where's the Fire Extinguisher? 72
37 Effective Communication 75
38 Focus on the Process, Not on the Outcome 78
39 Focus on Effort 80
40 Get To, Not Have To 82
41 There's Only One Game or Point That's Relevant 84
42 Eliminate Adjectives for Training and Competition 86
43 If You Don't Feel It, Act Like It 88
44 "Hire" a Constructive Coach 90
45 Chart Your Progress 92
46 Tell Yourself What You Want to Have Happen 94
47 Your Thoughts Make You Mad 96
48 You Can't Have Everything 99
49 The Only Failure Is a Failure to Learn 101
50 Regain Concentration on the Task at Hand 103
51 Practice as if It Is a Tournament 105
52 Success Is an Event; Excellence Is a Process 107
53 Pressure Doesn't Exist 109
54 Task Orientation vs. Ego Orientation 111
55 Thought Stopping 114
56 The Problem with Positive and Negative 116
57 Dispute the Stories You Tell Yourself 118
58 Accept Your Humanity 120
59 Human Being vs. Human Doing 123
60 In Your Body, in Your Target, or in Your Mind? 125
61 The Power of Neutral Thinking 127
62 Do Something . . . Anything! 129
63 Build a Case Before Making a Correction 132
64 I Care, but It Doesn't Matter 135
65 Anticipate vs. Expect 137
66 The Only Acceptable Expectations 139
67 Pace Yourself 141
68 The Role of Vision in Attentional Control 143
69 The First Domino 146
70 The Strongest Don't Always Survive 148
71 Play Your Highlight Reel 150
72 Trust Me . . . or Don't 152
73 Give 100% of Whatever You Have in Your Tank 155
74 "Fuck-It!" Mode 157

75 Courageous, Not Fearless . . . 159
76 Questions to Eliminate . . . 161
77 Mental Training vs. Education . . . 164
78 Check Tempo and Muscle Tension Under Stress . . . 166
79 Post-Execution Discipline Is Just as Important . . . 169
80 Post-Execution Grading . . . 171
81 We See the World Not as It Is but as We Are . . . 174
82 Be All That You Want to Be vs. All That You Can Be . . . 176
83 Raffle Tickets . . . 178
84 Accumulated Evidence . . . 180
85 Use Opportunities to Narrow Attention . . . 182
86 How to Spot a Toxic Relationship with Sport . . . 184
87 Be Your Best vs. Be the Best . . . 186
88 The System Matters More Than the End Goal . . . 189
89 Prioritize Decisiveness . . . 191
90 Lose Yourself to Find Yourself . . . 194
91 Fear Regret More Than Failure or Discomfort . . . 196
92 Take Advantage of "What Is" . . . 198
93 Eliminate Victim Mentality . . . 200
94 Work the Puzzle . . . 202
95 Develop a Mindset That Manages Uncertainty Well . . . 204
96 Fair but Not Equal . . . 206
97 Pizza and Chocolate . . . 208
98 Do Hard Things . . . 210
99 No End in Sight . . . 212
100 Own Your Role on the Team . . . 214
101 Scarcity vs. Abundance . . . 216
102 Beware of Interpretations . . . 217
103 Contemplation vs. Action . . . 219
104 Yes Mode vs. Maybe or No . . . 221
105 Sufficient vs. 100 Percent . . . 223
106 Don't Confuse Activity with Progress . . . 225
107 Develop a Healthy Perspective . . . 227
108 Who Do You Want to Be? . . . 229
109 Are You Willing to Suffer? . . . 231
110 Catch Yourself and Others Doing Things Well . . . 233
111 Ask for Input with a Beginner's Mindset . . . 235
112 Get It Right or Be Right? . . . 237
113 Reach the Ceiling or Raise the Floor? . . . 239
114 Go Be You . . . 241
115 Control the Second Thought . . . 243

116 Minimize the Time You Spend Looking in the Grass 245
117 Brain Budgeting 247
118 Be the Best Athlete for the Team 249
119 Intent Is Not the Same as Imperative 251
120 Share Your Mistakes 253
121 Impostor Syndrome 255
122 Respect the Game 257
123 Answer Your Rhetorical Questions 259
124 How Would You Act if the Outcome Was Certain? 262
125 Haunted by the Ghost of the Past 264
126 Progress Is Messy 266
127 Good, Better, How 268
128 Commit to Getting Clean Data 270
129 Are You the Hunter or the Hunted? 272
130 Get Clarity Around Personal Success Criteria 274
131 Get Distance from Yourself 276
132 What Is Under the Tree? 278
133 Swing the Club vs. Hit the Shot 280
134 Cocky or Confident? 282
135 Use Yesterday as Fuel 284
136 Come to Your Senses 286
137 Complete Your Compassion 288
138 Don't Let Preparation Go into Overtime 290
139 Build Strength Through Adversity 292
140 Name the Monster 294
141 Motivation Will Come and Go 296
142 You Are Your Most Important Opponent 298
143 The Game Cares What You Do, Not How You Feel 300
144 If You Put in X 302
145 Monitor Your Energy Expenditure 304
146 Appreciate the Success of Others 307
147 Gap vs. Foundation 309
148 How Would It Be to Face You? 311
149 Forget a Balanced Life 313
150 Squeeze Out the Last Drops 315

A Final Word on Trust and Commitment 317
Appendix: What's Holding You Back? 319
References 321
Acknowledgments 322
About the Author 323

FOREWORD

I first met Jeff Troesch through an ex-girlfriend. At the time I was ranked No. 1 in the nation in track and field's 800-meter event, and I had the honor of dating my female counterpart, one of the USA's best female half-milers. Jeff was helping her achieve her athletic potential, which I thought was nice, but I assumed sports psychology was not something that I needed. I mean, heck, I was already the best in the country!

But I didn't just want to be the best in my country, I wanted to be the best in the world.

Sadly, the relationship didn't last. Yet one of the first calls I made after the breakup was to Jeff: *Can you help me be better?* Thus began a partnership and a friendship that would reshape my life.

I had always assumed that sports psychology was just visualization and positive self-talk. While there are athletes who need to learn these skills, I did not struggle in these areas. Where I struggled most was in accepting and embracing the lifestyle of a professional distance runner. If I was happy off the track, I performed well on the track. Family issues, romantic relationships, business problems—these are all things I had to deal with off the track, and they had the potential to derail me mentally. Each time a new problem would creep up, Jeff and I would talk through the issue. I'd leave the conversation with a new mental framework and a *healthier* mindset, and I'd go on to crush my next workout or race.

Over the next few years Jeff helped me reframe my attitude toward my athletic career. I learned to enjoy the process and to put an emphasis on my daily goals (get sleep, eat healthily, have a good workout) rather than constantly obsessing over the long-term goals (winning medals). Of course, focusing on the little daily wins ultimately led to the big wins, as Jeff knew it would!

Jeff taught me how to control my emotions and harness some of my other weaknesses, even turning some of them into strengths. I am prone to mentally spiral when I feel something unjust has happened to me—for example, my agent messed up my travel, the meet director put me in the wrong hotel, an athlete who has previously tested positive for drugs is in my race. Unfavorable situations like these had a tendency to completely derail my entire race preparation. "You're going to defeat yourself before you even step on the track!" Jeff would say. And of course he was right. If I wasn't careful I would expend so much energy worrying about trivial problems that I would end up drained before the race even started.

I knew my issues were not unique—Jeff had seen them many times before in many other athletes. But he never tried to hit me with a one-size-fits-all manual. Instead he took the time to understand me as an athlete and as a person.

What makes this clock tick? I imagine Jeff asking himself that every time he meets a new athlete. No two athletes are alike; as such, there are no magic spells to make an athlete perform better. But what Jeff has put in these pages are as close to magic as you will find.

As you read *One Day Better* there will be little bits and pieces of wisdom that stick with you. I call these "Troesch nuggets," and I still carry many of them around with me today. In fact, I am writing this from Mount Everest Base Camp in advance of my attempt to summit the tallest mountain in the world. With each step I hear Jeff in my ear, "Control the things you can control, don't sweat the other stuff," "Roll with the punches the mountain gives you . . . "

These nuggets stay with you, they attach to your soul, and they are trying to tell you something. Listen to them, learn, and improve. Then go on to achieve your full potential—this is all that we can ask of ourselves on the playing field and in life.

NICK SYMMONDS

2-time Olympian

World Championship Silver Medalist

PREFACE

My entire life, I have been drawn to sports and the dynamics that exist beyond its physical and mechanical elements. Even as a young kid I was intrigued by how to optimize communication within teams, how to be an effective leader among my peers, and how to understand coach–athlete relationships. My curiosity was rewarded, as even before I started my professional consulting career, people sought me out for input or advice. By the time I began pursuing my undergraduate degree in business administration at Washington State University in 1978, I was befriended by several student-athletes on campus despite the fact that I had long ago given up my own pursuit of higher-level athletics.

Upon my graduation, I was hired by the Seattle SuperSonics NBA franchise as an assistant Media Relations Director and soon became Director of Media Relations. This role thrust me into situations where I was interacting with members of the NBA on a daily basis—some of whom I befriended and became a confidant to. What was clear was that many of these high-profile athletes had nowhere "safe" to turn to talk about the challenges that they were facing on and off the court, and I was used in some capacity by several of them. When the SuperSonics were sold to a new owner, I was fired and told it was because I was "too close to the athletes."

When I returned to graduate school at Washington State, I pursued an advanced degree in counseling psychology, taking additional courses in sport and exercise psychology. This was at a time when there were only a handful of sport psychology degrees offered in the US, as in 1987 the profession was in its infant stages.

Fast-forward nearly forty years, and I have made a career out of leveraging my counseling psychology degree and my affinity for interacting with athletes. I feel as though I am reasonably unique in that all I have done is work with and alongside athletes, coaches, sports organizations, and an occasional corporate entity. I have not taught at a university, I have not written books (until now!), and I have not created materials or podcasts or manuals. What I *have* done is gotten in the trenches of athletic environments and labored alongside the many thousands of clients that I have been fortunate to meet and assist.

I have spent almost four decades developing expertise and gathering anecdotal data on how the best in the world have gone from good to great and observing how many of those who had similar aspirations never made it to their metaphorical mountaintop. I have seen those who had early success and "couldn't miss" at a young age flame out and never be heard from again. I have seen late-blooming, "no chance" young athletes on their inexorable climbs to achieving personal successes about which they hadn't even dared to dream. I have seen older athletes resurrect their careers for one last good ride, and I've seen younger, high-performing athletes forfeit their long-term potential because of poor habits, poor decisions, a lack of discipline, or a lack of clarity of direction.

I have worked with CEOs down through lower-level managers of Fortune 500 companies and small businesses. I have worked with everyday people—the "weekend warriors"—who are just looking to get a little better at their chosen avocation. I have worked with very young, aspiring athletes who were among the best in the world at their respective ages. I have worked with athletes who presented themselves as very average in their skill set when I first encountered them. I have also been fortunate to have accompanied the best of the best: multiple medal winners in a number of Olympic Games in a wide variety of sports, World Cup soccer winners, winners of the World Series in baseball, winners of the Super Bowl in football, NBA Championship winners, winners of NHL's Stanley Cup, winners of multiple majors in professional tennis on both the men's (ATP) and women's (WTA) tours, and multiple major winners on both men's (PGA) and women's (LPGA) golf tours.

To the best of my recollection, what follows is a list of the sports within which I have consulted: aerial skiing, alpine skiing, American football, Aquabike, archery, Australian football, auto racing, badminton, barefoot waterskiing, baseball, BASE jumping, basketball, beach volleyball, biathlon, big wave surfing, billiards, BMX, bodybuilding, bowling, boxing, cage fighting, Canadian football, chess, cricket, cross-country skiing, curling, cycling, decathlon, disc golf, discus, diving, downhill skiing, downhill mountain biking, equestrian, fencing, field hockey, figure skating, free diving, golf, gymnastics, hammer throw, heptathlon, high diving, high jump, horse polo, hurdles, ice hockey, jai alai, javelin, jiujitsu, judo, karate, kiteboarding, kitesurfing, lacrosse, long jump, luge, marathon, middle-distance running, motocross, open water swimming, pickleball, pole vault, powerlifting, racewalking, racquetball, rodeo events, rowing, shot put, snowboarding, soccer, softball, speed skating, sprint, squash, steeplechase, stock car racing, surfing, swimming, synchronized swimming, table tennis, target shooting, tennis, triathlon, triple jump, ultramarathon, volleyball, water polo, waterskiing, weight lifting, windsurfing, and wrestling.

Interestingly, while each and every sport presents its own unique challenges and opportunities, a large percentage of mental skills development have application in any sport experience.

I decided to write *One Day Better* because I have been blessed with a unique opportunity to be inside the room with (and inside the heads of) these high-achieving coaches, organizations, teams, and athletes. Generally speaking, when consulting with me, people are quite vulnerable and reveal their unedited truths, frequently sharing things that they don't reveal to others. It has been a humbling "peek under the hood" at what goes on inside the human element of the athlete development business.

This book may be disappointing to some who are looking for a "tell-all" about the athletes with whom I've worked. I do not name names in this book. In fact, ever since I started working with high-profile athletes back in the 1980s, I made a decision to never publicly reveal my clients. I encountered far too many athletes who were suspicious of the motives of the people in their "circle," as they often thought (sometimes rightly so) that others were using their fame and their name to market or promote themselves. Many people in my industry reveal who they work with, and I have no judgment around that. I just know that I've felt very comfortable letting clients know from Day One that I would not expose our relationship. If they felt inclined to share that we worked together, that was at their discretion, and I will remain true to that principle here.

After having so many people encourage me to write a book for so many years, why this book now? In accumulating interesting and useful information about sport performance since the 1980s, I wanted to make sure that the information I have gathered and learned was distributed. I wanted to share it in the event it could be useful to others in the future—whether mental coaches, athletic coaches, athletes, parents, or everyday people. Much contained here has been helpful to me and to so many with whom I've worked in the past. I did not want these lessons learned to just vanish when I one day leave the world of mental training. My fervent desire is that the lessons will be found useful by those who read them.

INTRODUCTION

The world of sport has expanded its understanding and acknowledgment of the powerful role of an athlete's mentality and adopted a greater acceptance and appreciation for the impact of mental skills training. However, when I listen to broadcasters, sports fans, and everyday people extol the mental virtues of professional athletes, I find it comical that these athletes are attributed innate characteristics and strengths, as if the athlete was just *born to be great*. Roger Federer, who many would argue was one of the top tennis players of all time, was notable for his stoicism on the court and his seemingly unflappable disposition. However, if you pick up his own account of the development of his mental discipline in his autobiography, *The Master*, you can read the reference wherein "Federer is widely perceived as a 'natural,' and yet he is a meticulous planner who has learned to embrace routine and self-discipline."

These athletes were not gifted with some exceptional ability to perform under pressure—their abilities and skills have typically been trained and honed intentionally and purposefully. These same skills that guide champions to the pinnacles of their respective sports are the same skills that also provide essential foundations for the leaders in business, in industry, in medicine, and in virtually every other aspect of professional or personal life. These skills can be learned and practiced and acquired.

If you hired me to work with you, I would likely begin the process by having you complete a short assessment on your ability to navigate a variety of challenges—you'll find it (What's Holding You Back?) in the appendix. This can help jump-start our work, as the client usually presents in rough form the pertinent topics that they would like to prioritize in our work. From there, I generally meet with clients initially on a biweekly or monthly basis for a short period of time to narrow our work to the specific challenges that are unique to their situation. Early on, the process involves education and exploration of many of the concepts found in this book. We then work toward building strategies for implementation, feedback loops to check the effectiveness of what is being worked on, and guidance on how to continue to practice and train these concepts. Ultimately, we are amassing the reps required to establish intentionally applied strategies, behaviors, or habits.

As a mental performance specialist, there are also times when I'm asked to assist in a personal or corporate "crisis" to help guide an individual, team, or organization through strategies and steps to defuse a volatile situation and assist with restabilizing. However, even in these highly consequential situations, the concepts contained within this book are helpful and impactful.

Some elements of this book will not be applicable to you. This reality is in stark contrast to my effort over the years to make every interaction with my clients distinctly meaningful, customized, and applicable. Because I am not sitting with you, making observations, and tailoring the process to your unique challenges, it's up to you to review each concept thoughtfully and with an open mind to determine whether or not it is applicable or helpful to you. *One Day Better* is a toolbox, and it's your job to determine which concepts might work most effectively in the situation that presents itself uniquely to you.

Many of these concepts overlap, and we will repeatedly revisit a topic like attentional control or improved confidence, considering different angles. You will notice common denominators, such as being intentional with getting quality repetitions in training, working on being present through mindfulness or attentional training, and changing internal self-talk to improve stress tolerance and reduce triggering anxiety or distractibility.

I have been purposeful in not being overly directive or prescriptive with these concepts. Lasting, impactful mental performance acquisition is not one-size-fits-all, nor is it a simple proposition of following five easy steps. You will find a plethora of mental training "packages" that promise growth and improvement through platitudes, generalizations, and "quick-fix" promises. In contrast, I am hoping you will embark on an effort to successfully unpack your thoughts and emotions, leaning into the specificity, nuances, and tension that can be understood by you and managed differently. How these concepts apply to you, what they mean for you, is uniquely individual and comes from within each person. I intend to assist you by offering useful insights and increased awareness, rather than just deliver interesting information.

I want *One Day Better* to instigate and inspire your own internal exploration and contemplation. I suggest that you read no more than two or three concepts at a time and it's not necessary to read in a particular order. In consulting with athletes, I suggest just a couple of concepts at a time to facilitate reflection or application. As you reflect on a particular concept, consider:

- Are there areas of opportunity for greater awareness and discovery?
- Is there an opportunity for growth through application?
- How might this concept have been helpful to you in a previously encountered situation?

- How might this concept potentially be helpful in something that you are currently experiencing or are likely to experience in the future?
- How might you expand your knowledge about this particular concept outside of this book?

My greatest joy related to this project would be to learn that the people who have purchased it have highlighted multiple sections and scribbled notes in the margins, and discussed these ideas with their families, teams, or co-workers.

Despite the simplicity in many of these concepts, I also want to acknowledge how difficult it can be to implement them. I teach and work with these concepts every single day, and many of them remain a work in progress for me. I continue to have a difficult time "walking my talk" with several of these principles. Most of these concepts are about *becoming* rather than *arriving*—there is not an actual landing point that constitutes finality, perfection, or "The End." Self-actualization and growth are meant to be a lifelong pursuit, and the real challenge is to remain engaged for the entirety of your life. It's my sincere hope that a handful of these ideas might inspire your own growth, healthy change, and insight, somehow enhancing the quality of your life.

1

ONE DAY BETTER

"ONE DAY BETTER" IS THE HALLMARK OF A GROWTH MINDSET. It is all about your path toward mastery or excellence, which is not necessarily the same as you working toward achieving an outcome.

Early in my career I was focused on helping athletes and clients develop and work toward achieving SMART goals. The idea of Specific, Measurable, Attainable, Relevant, and Time-Oriented goals was among the concepts that I was taught in graduate school as foundational to the toolbox of a mental performance coach and subsequently their clients. But as time went on, I began paying more attention to what my clients were teaching me. I noticed that many of the individuals I was working with were constantly anxious about the gap between where they were that day and where they thought they needed to be in relation to their goals. A lot of them seemed relieved by the challenge I gave them to bring a little more each day, adding a little more wisdom or experience to their developmental process. Thus, I started speaking to the notion of getting a little better each day, with clear intention of the daily gains and an acknowledgment of those gains at the end of the day. This idea seemed to keep athletes appreciating their small daily "wins" and kept them on track toward what they were attempting to master.

In the years since, studies have shown that there is little evidence to support the idea that SMART goals enhance performance. There are many other paths to the top of the mountain.

I invite you to embark on a sustained effort to be one day better, every day.

There are a lot of similar refrains in the echelons of mental training, such as the concept of being 1 percent better each day. Mental training requires specificity and accuracy, so I don't like this 1 percent goal. Obviously, you cannot expect to be 100 percent better in 100 days—you could conceivably be 100 days better, but it's unlikely that you will be 100 percent better.

Rather than worrying about whether you'll be good enough two years from now to achieve a two-year goal, you can work to be 730 days better. If in 730 days you have made 730 days of progress, then you've done absolutely all that you can. It's going to be as "good" as it could possibly be in that time frame. Is that "good enough" to satisfy your goal? You'll find out in 730 days! Make this your intention and focus your energy on what is right in front of you today.

Here's how you can put it into practice. Approach the day with an intention of what you will do. At the end of the day, ask yourself, *What have I learned?* On the days when things go well, that One Day Better mentality generates positive feelings and emotions, and the lesson is often readily apparent. However, there will be days when you didn't perform very well . . . maybe you underachieved or lost badly. Make the choice to accept what happened and work to translate it into wisdom. The days when things don't go well are still One Day Better days, once we look past the frustration or pain that nearly always accompanies a rough day, and we can extract a lesson about what didn't go well—and why. You are now wiser and more experienced than you were yesterday. Sometimes One Day Better feels nice, and sometimes it feels painful. Either way, if you apply the lesson to tomorrow's tasks, you are better than you were yesterday. That's as complicated as it needs to get unless you value a more formalized process. In that case, you can take daily notes and keep them in a phone or journal so you have a go-to place where you gather evidence about your progress. **Whatever your daily experience, there is a lesson to apply going forward—you are one day wiser. Start again tomorrow with the renewed intention to be better than the day before.**

2

COMMIT TO MASTERY

ANY TIME YOU ARE LEARNING A NEW SKILL, THERE ARE STAGES to its acquisition. Bringing awareness to this process helps an individual to progress toward mastery.

There is a popularized learning model known loosely as the Model of Conscious Competence. Purportedly, it first appeared as a concept in the early 1960s, and for decades it was taught in a variety of settings to assist in understanding how people learn skills and advance toward mastery. There are different nuances, but it is generally taught as four stages. In the early days of my career, while working with colleagues on the development and evolution of new approaches to mental skills training for athletes, we utilized this concept but created what we felt was a crucial interim step in the process that helped us describe what we were experiencing in observing athlete and team skill development. The five-stage process that we developed follows:

1. Unconsciously Incompetent: You are not very good, and you don't know why. In this beginning stage there are innumerable things you don't know yet, and sometimes you don't know what you don't know! Even the things you do know are initially clumsy, difficult, and often confusing and challenging.

2. **Consciously Incompetent:** You are starting to know why you are not yet good at what you do. This next stage is when you are still not proficient, but you are gaining clarity on what to work on. In sport, this is often the late beginner to moderately skilled stage and is characterized by the athlete addressing specific deficient areas of skill and likely "bulk practicing" to get multiple repetitions to build competency.

3. **Unconsciously Competent:** You are good at what you do but not fully aware of how you generate competency on a regular basis. This is the interim step to which I alluded above. Many athletes with reasonable skill sets and competencies are unaware of the mechanisms in place that help them prepare optimally and/or perform well. When pressed, often these athletes are unable to give concrete answers about how they have achieved their level or how they were successful in a practice or competition. This is exemplified when an athlete will look puzzled or uncertain about why they are as good as they are or did as well as they did and perhaps respond:

> "I just woke up feeling great today."
> "I don't know what happened today—it all just clicked."
> "I can't believe that went so well—I'm not sure why."

This is the point when, in my professional experience, a lot of athletes seek out someone like me to be a part of their team and help them identify the specific variables that make them play well so they can replicate their successes intentionally and as often as possible.

4. **Consciously Competent:** You are good at what you do, and you are also aware of the mechanisms or systems you want to put into place to optimally prepare for competition or to compete in a more consistent

and conscious fashion. You know how to "get yourself there" and how to sustain competency—making adjustments if things start to falter.

5. Unconsciously Consciously Competent: Your technique, skill, or knowledge is now engrained, completely habitual. You are unconsciously executing with competency, with efficiency, and with ease. An easy analogy here is the example of driving a car. Most people get to a level of proficiency and competency where they remain unconscious to the slight adjustments of the steering wheel, brakes, and gas pedal that are occurring at all times. The skill becomes "automatic" and very little thinking is required in order to be reasonably successful. This is the ultimate state to which athletes aspire, and many highly skilled athletes do find themselves at times in this "flow" state when they are simply executing and not actively thinking about it.

Like many aspects in our practice, this is simple but difficult. Many individuals begin the progression and never become unconsciously consciously competent. Most people stop at step 3—unconscious competence. For these individuals, exhibiting competency will be inconsistent and intermittently out of their control.

What are the mechanisms that help you achieve the highest level of competency? At the higher levels of sport and business, there are many people who operate at step 4, conscious competence, with consistency. They can extract information from their daily experiences that makes them aware of how they generate competence—they are clear about the ways in which they are One Day Better.

Make it your goal to progress toward conscious competence. Mastery looks different for each of us, but it always starts with a high level of awareness and a willingness to extract and apply the lessons learned as skills and competencies are being developed.

3

EFFECTIVE VS. RIGHT

OVER NEARLY FOUR DECADES OF CONSULTING WITH ATHLETES, I've learned the importance of differentiating *right* from *effective*. **There is no one "right" way to do anything.**

As I have witnessed, there is no one right way to do mental training. There is no one right way to exercise or get fit. There is no one right or proper way to train technically, mechanically, or tactically. There is no one right technique or one right way to eat properly or recover optimally. Instead of trying to do it "right" or get it "right," I want the clients with whom I work to train and develop and compete in the ways that are most effective—for them.

The Halls of Fame in virtually every sport demonstrate that there is not a simple or singular formula for how to be successful. There are dozens of different golf swings and putting strokes among the all-time best golfers. The great pitchers in the game of baseball have used a broad spectrum of methods to rise to the top of their craft. There are multiple examples of highly successful athletes with unconventional shooting styles in basketball, field hockey, water polo, and lacrosse. There is a plethora of running forms among international champions in track and distance racing. The list could go on and on.

I want each and every athlete to approach the task at hand being less concerned about getting it right and more focused on learning what is effective for them. A large majority of the athletes I have worked with have been extremely high achievers in multiple arenas, not just in sports. Many approach most everything in their lives in a way that is borderline perfectionistic, which can manifest as being distracted and worried about getting something wrong or being fearful to make a decision or try something new. They want to know they're going to get it right before they are willing to make changes.

Instead, I encourage athletes and coaches to be open-minded to the idea that it's their job to figure out what's most effective for them. This is only discovered through trial and error, through failing and learning—and through experiencing success and having an accurate understanding of how that success was achieved. Only then can an intentional attempt to replicate those successes happen. Through this process, the athlete homes in on an awareness of what works best for them.

4

MENTAL DISCIPLINE MATTERS MORE THAN TOUGHNESS

MENTAL TOUGHNESS IS A COMMONLY USED CATCH-ALL PHRASE to describe certain characteristics associated with training and competing when it is difficult. Many athletes don't feel "tough" and aren't sure how to exhibit mental toughness traits. It can come as a huge relief to some of my clients to find out that I am not necessarily concerned about or interested in how tough they can be. In my experience, an athlete doesn't necessarily have to feel tough in order to manage challenges well. The construct of mental discipline is the common denominator.

Mental discipline is more valuable than toughness. There are plenty of people, myself included, who might be considered "soft" or not tough and yet they are incredibly disciplined. Just as an athlete is asking themselves to be disciplined with their technique or mechanics, I am also advocating that being disciplined mentally is how one generates a consistent internal environment.

One of the most basic and foundational elements of all that I teach is the notion that **our actions are often influenced by our emotions or feelings, and our feelings are nearly always triggered by our thoughts.** It looks like this:

THOUGHTS → FEELINGS → BEHAVIORS

This chain reaction is set in motion when something happens and we process it by thinking about it or evaluating it, have feelings about it, and then act accordingly. The key takeaway here is that circumstances and situations don't create feelings. Often, what creates feelings and emotions is how we choose to interpret what we're experiencing. When the ref makes a bad call, it doesn't make you mad. It's what you think about what the ref should have done that results in anger. Missing a shot or making an error doesn't create frustration. It's your thoughts about it that generate the frustration. It is not that your emotion is unwarranted, but for better or worse, your thought patterns helped to create that emotion.

Mental discipline requires that we learn to become less reactive and choose to respond in a disciplined manner. It is helpful to slow the process down, examine our thinking, and respond with intelligence and intention.

My recommendation is often to work this model backward in order to have greater insight and understanding. In other words, first examine a particular behavior (e.g., my putting stroke was quick, my racket speed slowed down, I didn't follow through on my shot), and then examine the emotion that might have preceded it (e.g., I felt nervous, I was underconfident, I was scared).

What were the thoughts that preceded the emotions?

I have to make this putt.
I can't keep missing my forehand.
If I miss this shot, we might lose.

These thoughts are the ones that created a domino effect that contributed to poor performance.

Through a disciplined approach to changing those thoughts in those moments, we are able to direct our thoughts into actions that give us a better chance for success.

Of course I'd like to make this putt—let's put a good stroke on it and feel the speed.
I want to rip my forehand with full racket speed—this gives me the best chance to hit a good shot.
I will make sure to feel a good leg bend and follow through on my free throw.

These are just some examples that might be helpful for a golfer, tennis player, or basketball player.

Ultimately, it is not just being "tough" in those situations; it's being disciplined with the internal environment that helps you as an athlete act in the way that is most likely to bring success.

5

RESPONSE ABILITY

WE HAVE THE ABILITY TO RESPOND IN ANY WAY WE CHOOSE to any circumstance we find ourselves in. So, when people talk about taking responsibility, I use wordplay to help them understand their ability to respond—their "response ability."

Generally speaking, in sport there will often be talk about how the officials did something, or how my opponent did this, or how my coach or teammate did that. **Regardless of what happens, you still have the ability to respond to any circumstance in any way you choose.** This is why I want to make sure everyone with whom I work takes ownership and responsibility and exercises their ability to respond.

When people don't recognize their options, their ability to adapt and adjust to whatever circumstance just befell them, they sometimes will end up playing the victim. They won't feel like they're in control of their next steps. In reality, there are things you can take control of, but it's easy to be distracted by things that can't be controlled—what just happened to you, why it happened, or who was to blame. An athlete might even internalize a situation and their own role in it—they are so frustrated about what they did that they don't recognize that they have an opportunity to pivot and make an adjustment. It's common to get caught up in anger or frustration—and in emotions rather than action.

When you're in the middle of a competition and you feel mad or frustrated, that reaction distracts you from the all-important question: *What do I do next?* It's a question that demands an intelligent and thoughtful response, not an emotional response.

Understanding your emotions is a part of life and sport. Emotions can often influence your response, but we want to minimize that influence. You want your response to be intentional so you can take full advantage of circumstances over which you have some influence or control.

If you withdraw and feel sorry for yourself or point the finger at someone else, how is that helping you get better? How is that improving your circumstances? Maybe it temporarily satisfies something inside of you, but it probably doesn't help you move in the direction you want to go.

To better facilitate our ability to respond rather than simply react, it helps to create a gap between what happens and our response. When we create space between the stimulus and the response, we can be more thoughtful about how we choose to respond. As human beings, we are all likely to have some deficits in this area. On a day-to-day or hour-by-hour basis, be intentional about responding rather than reacting, about being thoughtful rather than emotional. Specific practice around this is foundational to the mental skill development that leads to more consistently applied mental discipline.

6

TRUST VS. COMMITMENT

WOULDN'T YOU LIKE TO BE SO CONFIDENT IN YOUR GAME THAT you could simply "trust your swing" or "be loose and pass it" or "free it up," as many of my fellow mental-game gurus would advocate? Sure, it sounds good in theory, but how do you trust your swing or pass or shot if you're struggling? How do you trust you're going to make this putt if you've missed four just like it in the lead-up to this moment? How do you trust you're going to make a good pass if you've turned it over on your last two possessions? How do you trust your shot if you've missed your last three attempts? The answer is: *You don't need to trust.*

I'd like you to have trust, and I'd love it if all the athletes with whom I work trusted their execution in those moments completely. This would make their minds less cluttered, create less worry, and probably inspire them to new heights of confidence and success. However, virtually 100 percent of the athletes with whom I've worked have times when they don't trust one aspect of their game or another. That's when commitment becomes important.

Committing to a plan of action, a shot selection, or a tactic, and then actually executing in that moment with authority, helps develop trust. Without commitment, there is the tendency to be mentally distracted, have doubts, and second-guess yourself prior to executing. While the full trust that "all will be well" may not be achieved, with commitment you give yourself the best chance for something good to happen.

Former PGA Tour golfer Payne Stewart said, "Better to commit to the wrong thing in golf than to be uncommitted to the correct thing." So, how can you implement this notion into your game? If you are in between clubs on a shot, pick one, be decisive, and commit fully to that choice. If you aren't sure if changing your tactic during your tennis match or swim meet is the right choice, make the commitment to execute assertively so you can get feedback on whether or not what you've decided upon works. Begin to recognize how many times you've executed your task without being committed and challenge yourself to pull the trigger with full commitment—independent of whether or not you "trust it" yet.

Each time you're in your competitive arena, you have an opportunity to get feedback about yourself as an athlete, and the most accurate feedback you'll receive comes from fully committing to your execution and then making adjustments for the future. This allows you to earn trust through repeated committed action. Without that, you may never trust certain aspects of your game, no matter how regularly you practice or play.

7

BE A SCIENTIST, NOT A JUDGE

APPROACH YOUR PERFORMANCE AS A SCIENTIST CONDUCTING an experiment. Best results rely on objectivity. A scientist gathering information is on a path of discovery. There is no good or bad, right or wrong. A scientist is striving for replicability or the ability to reproduce a desired result. Athlete development is no different—it's all about taking a rational look at the situation. *What did I observe or learn? What variables might I adjust to get clean data?* **Be neutral, objective, and as factual as possible.** This increases the likelihood of reproducing desired results.

In contrast, many athletes are constantly in judgment of their performance: *That was good, that was bad, that was right, that was wrong, that sucked, that was awesome.* They are living in their head, with judgment, emotionally invested in their performance.

Passion is undeniably part of sport, and used productively, it can trigger growth and dedication and achievement. Unchecked, however, it can compromise your ability to engage in rational thought. Instead of making observations from a position of neutrality, too much passion or excessive emotion can put you in judgment mode—before, during, and after the performance. Every outcome might then be assessed as *pass or fail*. Development and discovery are stunted by such a mindset, often before the game or event even starts.

To cultivate productive or successful performance, work toward being as neutral and objective and as factual as possible. *Is this something I want to continue, or is this something to minimize?* It's okay to be passionate and emotional, but take measures to remain rational and grounded in diligent observation.

Focus less on what others propose is right. Instead, emphasize an understanding of what works best for *you*. Doing this might allow you to become more adaptable, more receptive to learning what works for you, and less distracted or worried about judging whether it is right or wrong.

8

AWARENESS VS. ATTENTION

ATTENTIONAL CONTROL AND ATTENTIONAL SHIFTING CAN BE taught and trained, and these skills have enormous value for athletes in every sport and at every level.

We start with precise language that makes the subtle but important distinction between attention and awareness. This distinction is appreciated primarily as it relates to outcomes, results, and achievement goals. Let me clarify.

When I'm driving an athlete's attention toward the process or the task of what they're involved in versus putting their attention on the result, they might initially balk at this idea:

"Winning is all that matters."
"I've been told to set result-oriented goals my whole life."
"It's all about getting the 'W' in the end."

I tell athletes that I am in the business of winning. I understand how important it is to earn the scholarship, get drafted, or retain one's contract. I also understand that quite often, these desired goals are accomplished through achieving results. Here's the slight adjustment in thinking that I'm suggesting: **Retain awareness of the desired**

outcomes, results, or goals, but make sure your moment-to-moment attention is in the present and focused on the immediate task that's in front of you.

Having an *awareness* of how you'd like things to turn out today or this year, or to what heights you'd like to take your career, is fine as a guidepost—something you are aware of and inspired or motivated by—but don't put your full *attention* on these things. The highly demanding environment of competitive sports requires that an athlete's attention be placed on being in the present and executing their task. The difference between these concepts might feel slight at first, but the distinction is significant.

Feel free to have momentary awareness of how you'd like things to turn out in the end, then lock in with your attention to give yourself the best opportunity to manifest the outcome you're craving.

WIN is an acronym that is popular among mental performance coaches and athletes—*What's Important Now*. This is a good real-time reminder to bring your attention back to the thing that is the highest priority in this moment and to be disciplined in keeping your focus on the task at hand. While your immediate outcome and long-term goals are certainly important, let's work toward your attention being on what is relevant. This is the immediate undertaking right in front of you.

9

HAVE A PURPOSE IN MIND

OFTENTIMES ATHLETES WILL GO INTO A PRACTICE WITH A less-than-clear intention about what success looks like. This is a missed opportunity. Ask yourself, *In what ways am I going to get better today? What are my success criteria?* A purpose-driven approach allows people to be more efficient, energized, focused, and on task.

This remains true regardless of whether the athlete is training alone or showing up to a coached session. Even in team sports, the athlete takes ownership of their own development. Don't simply show up looking to the coach to tell you what to focus on. Of course you will follow your coach's agenda, but your growth is not entirely dependent on a coaching relationship. Each day is an opportunity to take ownership of your evolution and to hit micro goals that work toward the achievement of macro goals. Tennis great Rafael Nadal has acknowledged in multiple interviews how important it was to him that he held himself accountable in every single training session to make sure he had clarity of purpose and intention before stepping onto the tennis court for a competition.

If your intention today is to really make sure that your effort is optimized in whatever you're doing, then anything the coach puts in front of you or anything the training log says you're to do is likely to be better executed because you are invested in that purpose. Another benefit of having a purpose in mind is that it allows you to make use of arbitrary training sessions or things that don't seem to connect. **If your purpose is to optimize your effort, anything put in front of you is an opportunity to get better.**

10

FOCUS ON **WHAT TO DO,** NOT WHAT IT MEANS

WE HAVE A TENDENCY TO PUT OUR ATTENTION ON THE CON-sequences of things, or the implications of things—what they're for or what they're about—as opposed to focusing on what to do. Take basketball, for example. Let's say you're at the free throw line and you look at the scoreboard. You see the time remaining on the clock and note that your team is down one point and there are twenty seconds left in the game. You are likely to think, *If I make these shots, this will happen. If I miss these shots, that will happen.*

This often creates a distraction from the task at hand. You know what to do, but where is your attention? When you start thinking about possible outcomes and/or consequences, it takes your attention away from the purity of executing the skill or task.

Making this putt means I win the club championship.
Missing this putt means I don't go to the US Open.

This is thinking about what the putt means, its implications or consequences. What is your task? What do you do now?

I'm going to roll this putt with great speed toward the hole.

Put your attention toward the task or the process—what to do. What you are asking your body to do in those situations is not different than what you ask your body to do in training every day. It can just feel different because your attention is drawn toward what it's "for" rather than drawn toward the elements of execution.

Sports commentators constantly emphasize what's at stake for an athlete or team, saying things like, "This is a critical situation. If he is successful here, this is what will happen." Even as a fan, you are likely to be focused on the consequences or implications of a moment, but for the athlete, these things are completely irrelevant to the task of executing the skill right now.

Outside of the competitive arena, athletes can be easily distracted by social media:

What did that win mean?
How many likes did my post get?
How much did I sign for, and what did that other athlete get?

All of these things will pull you away from *task orientation*—doing your job and continuing to advance toward excellence. This is the most productive place to direct your attention—in or out of your competitive environment.

It's not like we're going to eliminate what something means, but we can minimize how much attention and power we give to what it means. You really want to win? No kidding. You really want to get the prize? You really want to cash that big check? Of course you do! Now let's put your attention on what to do to give yourself the best chance to get what you want.

11

BELIEF, DECISIVENESS, AND COMMITMENT

WHEN I CONSULT WITH A PARTICULAR GROUP OF ATHLETES and coaches for an extended period of time, we eventually delve into some interesting and subtle nuances pertaining to their thoughts and perceptions of their sport experience. These conversations necessitate that a concept be "sliced very thinly," as the exact situation or precise meaning of what we are talking about can sometimes be difficult to clearly articulate. Sometimes it is challenging to be completely certain that both parties are talking about the same construct. This is why I am a proponent of making sure we have agreement on the exact words we're using and how these specific words depict a particular type of thought or notion.

Case in point, let's tease out the distinctions between *belief*, *decisiveness*, and *commitment*. An athlete might say, "I want to have more belief." I consider *belief* to be the athlete's thoughts either around how they see themselves capable of performing well in a general sense or how they see themselves actually performing well in a particular situation. For some athletes, belief is a challenge, and improving belief is important work to undertake.

There are other athletes who have a reasonable level of belief, but their true challenge is *indecisiveness*. I have worked with thousands of Division 1 collegiate student-athletes, many of whom are very intelligent. Some of these athletes really struggle being willing to make decisions in a timely fashion because they want to "get it right." They often hesitate to pull the trigger on an answer because they are worried it might not be correct and are constantly striving to "get an 'A'" on their test—whether it be in the classroom or the athletic arena. A reasonable percentage of my professional client base faces the same challenge. They might have belief, but they are hesitant or tentative because of indecisiveness—sometimes their skill set provides too many options!

Finally, there is the concept of commitment, which I speak about throughout this book. The commitment to which I refer here is not the long-term type of commitment to a process or toward a goal; here, *commitment* refers to acting assertively and intelligently in a moment of execution. An athlete might have belief, might be decisive, and still might hesitate through the execution/impact zone of a golf swing, a baseball swing, a volleyball serve, or a javelin throw.

When an athlete, coach, or businessperson is able to articulate the exact challenge they face in those moments of execution, it provides tremendous insight that can be used to work toward improving their belief, decisiveness, or commitment with a more deliberate plan of attack.

12

BE HERE NOW

THE GREAT TENNIS PLAYER ARTHUR ASHE SAID IT BEST: "Start where you are, use what you have, do what you can."

Work toward being present in whatever you are doing—not only physically, but mentally. In either case, be here now, not wishing you were somewhere else.

I often find that clients with whom I've worked are haunted by ghosts from their past. They will say,

> "Before my injury, I could lift more weight," or
> "Before I got older, my pace was faster."

Okay, we can acknowledge that's where you were then, but where are you now?

Other clients are fixated on the future, so much so that wishing becomes their strategy.

> "I wish I had . . ."
> "I wish I wasn't . . ."

Wishing is a terrible strategy. What do you have to work with? How can you leverage and take advantage of where you are now? Do the best you can with what you have and where you are right now.

When I talk about being here in this moment, it's easy to understand, but it's difficult to employ this moment as an actionable space. **Let go of the past and the future and the internal distraction they bring, causing you to think about what you can't do or forcing you to spin a fairy tale.**

Increase your awareness of when your mind wanders to the past or leapfrogs into the future. Gently return to the moment that you're in. What can you do in the here and now?

13

DEVELOP **ROUTINES** AND RITUALS

ONE OF THE CHALLENGES IN MENTAL TRAINING IS TO KEEP your attention on the most productive thing at the most productive time. Most great athletes get their minds, or their internal environments, to be in a consistent place by building routines or rituals that prepare a place for them to basically park their attention when it might be prone to wander. They establish a consistent place to go to in between points, in between shots, or in between pitches in a micro sense—or in between games, in between matches, or in between competitions in a macro sense.

There's some comfort for athletes in knowing where they can bring themselves back to if they find themselves in a mind space that is nonproductive or unhelpful. **Most great athletes have routines that help them develop a consistent internal environment, which they then impose upon their competition or on their training session.** Athletes with a less developed mental perspective allow their external environment to influence their internal environment, and by that point, they don't have an organized or structured way to bring themselves back to an internal consistency.

I will ask athletes, "How's your routine?"

They usually go on to describe in intricate detail the things they're doing physically. But I'm also talking about an internal routine. It's not just what their body is doing in between points—*I touch a towel, and then I take a breath, and then I move my feet into position*—or whatever it may be, every single time. While that might be the physical element of the routine or ritual, what's happening internally? Are they applying their attention in a consistent, routine fashion?

The model I use with athletes is a simple progression: *plan, commit, execute, reflect/recover*. By guiding your attention through each step, you can facilitate internal consistency as well as external consistency.

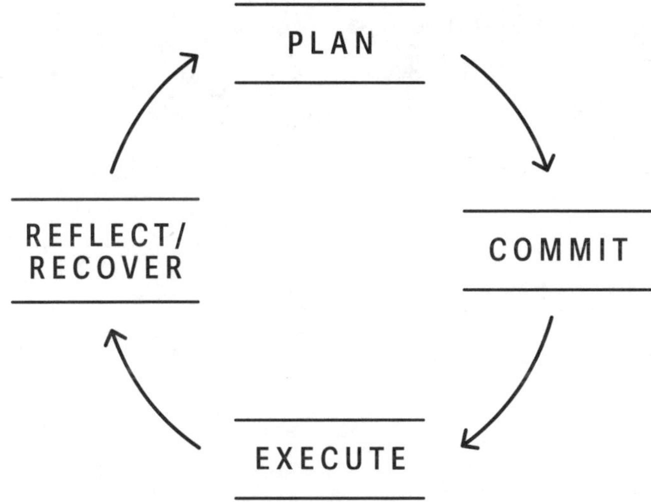

If we're talking about in between points, pitches, or golf shots, you plan for your shot, you commit to the shot, you execute the shot, you have post-execution reflection and recovery, and then you experience sort of a flushing mechanism of whatever happened last. This serves as a routine for managing your internal environment. Within each of these steps, you might also have a routine.

Let's say you're a golfer. What is the routine that helps you gather the requisite information in a deliberate fashion? What is the routine to get yourself to establish commitment pre-execution? For the reflection and recovery, your routine might look like this, as an example:

> Immediately post-execution, I have my human reaction.
> Then I ask, *What did I learn from that?*
> Next, I think about how to translate that into something tactical that I can bring to the planning of the next shot.

All of this factors into your routine in between shots or points. Every step of the way, you are bringing your attention to the most productive thing at the most productive time. Having a systematic approach for the downtime in between moments of execution can be incredibly valuable to help keep you on track and internally stabilized.

14

YOU CAN'T **STEAL SECOND** WITH ONE FOOT ON FIRST

IF YOU WANT TO GIVE YOURSELF A CHANCE TO BE GREAT, IT requires taking a risk. If you want to play it safe, you can have safety, but it's less likely to be the path to get you to excellence. Put simply, getting to second base demands that you step off of first.

Let's ground this platitude in reality to better understand how individuals inhibit their pursuit of excellence and what can be done about it. A tennis player is exceedingly worried about failing, terrified to make even a small mistake. The solution is not for this athlete to wait until they become fearless. **The true advantage lies in becoming more courageous in the face of fear.**

We might set a goal for her to come away from her next match having exhibited more courageous action than she did in the previous match. This might mean she is more aggressive on short ball opportunities to attack or more forceful with her second serve than she normally is. Certainly, you can have a desirable outcome without taking the risk. The tennis player might win her next match without more courageous action and by taking on more acceptable risk, but if she continues to let fear influence her play, she's much less likely to progress her game.

This concept plays out the same in every sport. When athletes compete tentatively or hesitantly, choosing fearful execution over courageous execution, and they happen to temporarily succeed, they feel lucky, not competent. They may realize, *I won the point, but not because I went after it.*

It's not enough to be lucky—luck can certainly help, but we don't want to rely on it as we pursue greatness. Resolve to be courageous enough to go after each point, even if it means failing, and learn to affirm and acknowledge courageous action even if, in that moment, it didn't produce the desired result.

Pulling in another metaphor, take your big sword into battle—don't hide behind a shield with a butter knife. Lacking bravery or courage, you are likely to walk away feeling lucky or regretful, not more confident. You give yourself your best chance to win the battle if you intelligently swing your big sword.

15

BREATHE

A LOT OF PEOPLE UNDERUTILIZE THE PHYSIOLOGICAL AND psychological benefits that come through taking a deep, intentional breath, or being intentional with breathing in general. It's deceptively simple, but if we're talking about an Ironman triathlete, it's not just one intentional breath—it's nine hours of being thoughtful about using their breath in a way that optimizes performance.

Depending on the sport or the circumstance, different types of breathing can be extremely valuable both physiologically and psychologically. Breathing can slow down the body's internal rhythms—including heart rate, respiration rate, and even blood pressure. Psychologically, breath work can ground an athlete in their body, which might be preferable to revving up their thinking brain. When your attention is on what you are physically feeling—particularly through your hands, or feet, or face—your brain attends to those sensations. Placing your attention on how your body feels literally slows down your brain-wave activity and can decrease the "flooding" of thoughts that might become disruptive. As an example, if I am deeply aware of how my breath feels in my nostrils as I inhale or how my stomach expands, I am much less likely to be distracted by my internal dialogue or chatter.

I like to help athletes visualize the value of breath work with a short video featuring a neuropsychologist who uses a wireless device to measure brain-wave activity in real time. We can watch the brain-wave activity be visibly minimized as the athlete takes a deep breath. So **not only does breathing affect the physiology of heart rate and the respiratory system; it literally shuts down excessive traffic in the brain** and shifts the activity to slower, calmer alpha waves, with a reduced volume of beta waves.

Utilization of breathing techniques calms the brain. Look for ways to incorporate breath work into your routines, both inside and outside of training.

16

DO YOU HIT THE **GAS PEDAL** OR THE BRAKES?

MAKING DECISIONS COMES RELATIVELY EASILY AND COMFORTABLY for some of us. For many others, decisions come with the strong tendency to question ourselves as soon as the decision has been reached.

Many coaches and athletes have a reflexive response toward some of their decisions that presents like "buyer's remorse"—the feeling of regret or worry after making a purchase.

If this is a familiar challenge for you, it can be extremely useful to work toward a habit of initiating action upon your decision as soon as is prudent so that you can more quickly flow from conclusion to action. This minimizes the time lag when you might be prone to question yourself, despite having spent adequate time considering your alternatives.

This is an exercise in reducing self-judgment and self-doubt and taking the calculated risk to act upon your own deduction. If this proclivity might be true for you, see if you can hit the gas pedal more quickly after you've come to your decision.

Of course, there are some who have the opposite challenge and may be overly spontaneous or impulsive with their decisions. This is a different circumstance, and these folks would do well to tap the brakes on action in select instances.

Size up where you fit in the continuum from "brake tapper" to "gas pedal pusher." Take some time to recognize if there are certain decisions where you act one way and other decisions where you have the opposite tendency. As with all things, **having clarity about your behavioral tendencies allows you to examine whether an adjustment would help you be more efficient or effective.**

17

APPROACH OR AVOID?

AMONG THE SIMPLEST YET MOST POWERFUL LESSONS TO BE learned as an athlete is related to how you choose to look at the situation that's in front of you.

In every circumstance and situation, you have the choice to see the place you're in as either an opportunity or a threat. Without delving into the details of how the brain functions, suffice to say that we are hardwired to reflexively recognize the threat in situations more naturally than we are to see the opportunity. Thus, for many, their initial take on circumstances is to focus on things they are trying to avoid.

"Don't want to hit it there."
"Don't want to lose to that guy."
"Can't miss on this attempt."
"Try not to make a mistake."

Examining your own tendencies in your sport (and life) experiences can help identify how your language can be changed and your focus can be redirected to what you *want* rather than what you're trying to *avoid*. For years, I've been alongside athletes in real time in the middle of their competitions, and I have worked relentlessly to guide them to reframing their perspectives so they are seeing the challenge and opportunity rather than just the dangers they're trying to avoid.

> "I know you don't want to hit it there, but where *do you want to hit it?*"
> "Of course you don't want to have that happen. *What can you do to increase the likelihood of getting what you want?*"

It is crucial that whatever role we are in at any particular time—as an athlete, as a coach, as a businessperson, as a parent—we do the difficult work to make sure we are clear about what we would prefer or what we would want to happen, and then be willing to go after what we want. **Going after what you want rather than being in a constant state of avoiding a negative outcome gives you the best chance for success.** Additionally, it increases the enjoyment factor while mitigating the natural stress that comes in many situations where uncertainty is present and failure is a potential outcome.

What would a good outcome look like in your situation? See it and then go after it!

18

LOOK AT THE TARGET...OR DON'T

AS STATED AT THE BEGINNING OF THIS BOOK, ONE OF THE PRIMARY and foundational philosophies I've developed over the years is a belief that there is no one "right" way to do anything—there is only an effective way to do something, and for individual athletes, there is often a slightly customized and unique way of being effective and successful.

This particular idea regarding target orientation is among those concepts rooted in the notion that there's no one right way to do anything. For some people, in some instances, putting their attention toward the target is what is most effective. For these people, it takes them out of worrying how to reach it. Their focus becomes more about *where* and less about *how*.

In the sport of baseball, for some hitters, thinking about hitting the ball into the right centerfield gap frees them up to do what they have already trained their body to do. In seeing the spot where they want the ball to go, they become less hung up on how to get it there. It goes without saying that there have been enough preparation reps prior to this moment, and the athlete has developed the requisite skill to carry out the task at hand. Having all of that in place, **some athletes find that being really attentive to the target can free them to go after it.**

> For the golfer, it's seeing the middle of the fairway and not overthinking how to hit the ball or eyeing the front edge of the cup over which they want to roll their putt.
> For the archer, it's seeing the bullseye, not thinking about how to get the arrow there.

This works for some as long as their target remains an intention, not an imperative.

Now, here come the caveats. For some people, being too target-oriented creates anxiety because they see the target as an imperative. Rather than looking at the target as an intention, when they are thinking, *I want the ball to go there*, their thinking becomes more of an imperative: *I have to get the ball to that target*. When this occurs, it's likely no longer as productive.

There's a need for yet another option, because some people exist more in their body as opposed to in their head. For these individuals, their execution will be more productive if they put their attention on what they are doing kinesthetically rather than at their target. For example, a hitter might think about or feel a simple point of execution such as, "I am loading into my right hip in my swing."

Golf psychology often champions the idea that golfers need to be target-motivated. While that may be true for some players, it is not true for all. As an example, I worked with a professional golfer who rose through the ranks to be No. 1 in the world. For that person, fixated attention on the target was not a viable strategy. Will it work for you? It depends—put it to the test and find out.

19

INCREASE THE ODDS

I ASK MY CLIENTS TO WORK DILIGENTLY TOWARD THEIR aspirations, knowing that there is no guarantee of any kind regarding outcomes. While this may seem like a downer, I remind athletes that it's their job to do everything within their power to increase the likelihood of success. I want them to be motivated to work intelligently, deliberately, and relentlessly to increase their odds.

From a macro perspective, no athlete has complete control over whether or not they will earn the all-star nod, get the scholarship, be selected in the professional draft, or sign the big contract.

More immediate questions come first:

Will I make the roster?
Will I be a starter?
Will I make the traveling team?

On the daily, you might ask, "Is making the choice before me going to ensure my success today? Is this next rep going to mean that I win?"

The answer to all of the above is clear: We don't know! All we do know and can know is that if you are clear about how to execute the task right in front of you, if you are clear about how to be a great teammate or student of the game, and if you match that insight and intention with requisite physical and mental skills (and a dash of luck!), you have increased your chances for outcome success.

It's as simple as that. Get comfortable with the notion of increasing your odds on a daily basis, and free yourself from the distractions about whether or not things will work out.

The best athletes in the world get comfortable with "I don't know how it's going to turn out," and then set about giving themselves the best chance to succeed.

20

ACE: SCORE THE CONTROLLABLES

"CONTROL THE CONTROLLABLES" IS A POPULAR CATCHPHRASE among coaches and athletes. I use the acronym ACE, as I believe *attitude, concentration*, and *effort* are all within our control. When an athlete or coach goes into a training session or a competition—or, more broadly, into whatever they're doing in life—**they can hold themselves accountable to optimizing their attitude, locking in and sustaining their concentration, and maximizing their effort.**

I will often have athletes score themselves at the end of a training session, where they get 10 points for each controllable. An ACE score of 30 would be a day where they optimized attitude, concentration, and effort. Furthermore, I want the athletes to grade themselves in each of those categories post-competition. We often see a high correlation between ACE scores and reasonable outcomes.

If you are a coached athlete or if you have a training partner, somebody you respect or trust, it can be helpful to have them score you as well. From there we can consider any dissonance between how you scored yourself and how the other people saw you—and maybe even have a discussion around that.

Sometimes a player will say, "Yeah, I put my attitude at a 6," and the coach will step in and say, "I see it as a 9 or 10." What was going on outwardly that caused the player's attitude to seem on point to the coach? Again, these are controllable variables that influence performance, as opposed to just looking at a number on the stopwatch. When we put tangible numbers to intangible elements of performance, we can better describe and discuss them.

21

EVERY REP **MATTERS**

THERE'S AN OPPORTUNITY TO LEARN SOMETHING IN EVERY rep you do, in whatever you're doing. When something hasn't gone the way you wanted it to go, there's information in that problem or failure or disappointment. There's something to extract—a "+1" in every situation.

If it takes 10,000 reps or 50,000 reps or 1 million reps of something to master it, even the reps that were painful or didn't work very well are still valuable. **We learn through not just the things that work well, but also through the things that don't work.**

Watch a young child learning to walk and you will notice how every time they fall down, they're learning something about balance. It is nonsensical to think that the child only learns from the steps taken successfully and not from the falling down.

As it relates to anything in sport, we have a tendency to get so frustrated with the disappointments or the problems that we sometimes fail ourselves by forfeiting the lesson that is available. The lesson is always there—it's just a matter of whether or not we choose to identify it, extract it, and utilize it.

22

WHAT WILL YOU DO **NEXT TIME?**

ONE OF THE MORE VALUABLE SKILLS DEVELOPED BY ELITE performers is the ability to quickly apply what they learn. After a training session, after competitions, or in the middle of their practices and/or games, athletes who "get it" are constantly attuned to what is happening so they can absorb it and use it as soon as possible.

Develop a brief check-in immediately after execution to identify what was learned and what to do next time. Making this a habit will take some time and commitment. **Literally train yourself to reflexively say, "Next time . . ." Fill in the blank with what you want to repeat or how you want to adjust.**

> Immediately after an at bat, a baseball hitter could say, "Next time pick up the spin of the ball earlier."
> Immediately after a serve, a tennis player might say, "Next time be a little more aggressive with your follow-through."
> Immediately after hitting a golf ball, a golfer could say, "Next time, feel that same feeling in your tempo—that was great!"

In every sport, in multiple situations, there are chances to direct your attention to the next time you will encounter a similar opportunity. Using intentional self-talk to take advantage of these micro lessons can be the difference between success and failure in the short term, as well as realizing your full athletic potential in the long term.

23

ELIMINATE THE SHOULDS, NEEDS, AND HAVE-TOS

PRECISE LANGUAGE IS EXTRAORDINARILY IMPORTANT IN mental training and mental discipline. Certain words influence our internal environments in a way that is nonproductive. When we tell ourselves what we *should* do, what we *need* to do, what we *have to* do, what we *must* do, what we're *supposed* to do, all of those statements are externally imposed actions that can place excessive demand on athletes.

What's more, they often generate anxiety. The part of the brain that is action-oriented is triggered—cued up to do that thing we "have to" do. Simultaneously, the threat center of the brain gets fired up. It begins processing the consequences—*What happens if I don't do it?* This interplay goes on in the brain, and ultimately, it leaks into the stress center. As a result, we often experience muscle tension and worry.

It is important to make a distinction between a competitive constraint and a self-imposed stressor. For example, if you're a basketball player, it is factually accurate that if your team is behind by two points with a few seconds left in the game, your team "has to" score in order to tie or win the game. That is a competitive constraint. However, if you are telling yourself throughout the game that you "have to" make a basket or "must" stop the other team from scoring right now, these are self-imposed stressors which are not factually accurate.

Alleviating the problem is a matter of changing "shoulds" and "needs" and "have-tos" to more precise language. For example, early in the basketball game you don't *have to* score a basket on the next possession. You might change the language to address what you *want to* have happen here or what you know you're capable of doing. From there, it's a matter of "let's go see" if you can make that happen. This is very different from "I've got to" messaging.

Shift your mind away from an overload of self-imposed demands and threats so you can recognize an opportunity and feel more free and eager to respond.

24

BUILD A CALLUS

GET ENOUGH REPS IN TRAINING THAT WILL TRANSFER DIRECTLY into competition. A lot of times, people avoid doing the things they're not very good at, or they don't get in a lot of reps that are psychologically or emotionally demanding. We strengthen ourselves by getting quality reps, putting ourselves in uncomfortable situations so that we build a callus, effectively training toughness around certain psychological and physical elements.

If you use a shovel for a weekend and you haven't been shoveling much, you will develop blisters, not calluses. It's the same with psychological aspects of competition. If a person hasn't developed their emotional and physical resilience in training sessions, when they go into a competitive situation, those aspects of performance will be stressed and their limits will be tested. Oftentimes this is where athletes come up short—they lack the resilience and familiarity to manage situations well across a spectrum of circumstances. **Put in the time to build a callus, and you will be better prepared to respond in a critical moment.**

It is important to note that athletes can also take the reps and work ethic too far, grinding away at something to the point where they are no longer building a callus; the effort is now wearing down to the bone. Physical and psychological elements of preparation can be overdone, resulting in physiological fatigue, cognitive overload, or overtraining syndrome. Respect the limit but recognize that a commitment to consistent exposure to something that pushes you outside of your comfort zone can be beneficial.

25

WHAT TRIGGERS YOUR **ATTENTIONAL DRIFT?**

IN ALIGNMENT WITH THE CONCEPT OF SELF-DISCOVERY AND self-awareness, it can be valuable for athletes to be made aware of the types of situations, thoughts, or patterns that might exist that can influence an attentional drift—that is, when your mind wanders or is distracted away from where you want your attention and focus to be at any one moment.

Here are some of the questions you could ask to increase your awareness and understanding of what is happening:

- Is the distraction internal (e.g., thoughts or pictures) or external (e.g., noise, people talking, etc.)?
- If internal, what sorts of thoughts are distracting to you?
- If external, what is happening around you to influence your change in focus?
- Are there identifiable patterns that have historically influenced a higher likelihood for a loss of concentration? (For example, "When I am in the lead," "When a lot of people are watching," "When my opponent looks intimidating," etc.)
- Are the distractions things you can control?

- Are the distractions related to the quality of your performance? (For example, "I'm playing so well/bad right now.")
- Are the distractions related to the score or outcome of the competition? (For example, "I think I'm going to lose/win.")

An awareness of what sorts of situations might increase the likelihood of attentional drift can help you proactively prepare to employ attentional shifting strategies. Knowing your tendencies can help you more quickly engage your coping strategies and reset your attention.

Every athlete has their own unique challenges with attentional control, but the ones who are clear about what triggers their attentional drifts are more primed to respond well to those drifts and minimize any immediate damage done.

26

CURRENT EVENTS, NOT HISTORY

MANY ATHLETES FOCUS THEIR ATTENTION ON WHAT THEY DID most recently—whether it's their last turn at bat, or the last play, or the last shot. They are still attaching themselves to it, and they seem to want to put a lot of energy into what just happened. This can be true whether the previous moment was one that didn't go well or one that won the game!

In these situations, I find myself constantly refreshing people to the present moment. I don't want a history lesson. I'm interested in current events. I will say to an athlete, "So you played badly last week? Okay, I'm hearing that, but here you are. How do you take advantage of the situation you have right now?" Or, "That's great that your last tournament went so well! How do you leverage what you learned there and apply it today?"

In his Growing Leaders curriculum, Tim Elmore uses the analogy of keeping your focus on the windshield, not the rearview mirror. While it can be useful to glance in the rearview mirror when we are driving, we want to keep the majority of our attention on what's right in front of us. **By putting less emphasis and energy on what happened "back there" and more emphasis and energy on the opportunity in front of you, you can be more present and productive.**

27

INCORPORATE **RECOVERY** INTO YOUR ROUTINE

RECOVERY HAS A MEANINGFUL ROLE TO PLAY, BOTH ON THE macro and micro levels. The very concept of periodization is meant to ensure that what a person does on the macro level allows time and space for real rest and recovery. This means an athlete will permit themselves to pull away from their sport experience or training for a period of time, acknowledging that these breaks support performance gains in the months and years ahead.

I've spent much of my career working alongside student-athletes, who often have multiple, even competing, goals. It could be that they are studying for a big exam or boards while they're in a routine of putting in a certain level of effort on their sport. People sometimes get caught up in trying harder and doing more, and for some it means they miss the opportunity to recharge their battery. This can be a result of many things: an attempt to try to do too many things at once, a misimpression that "more is always better," an anxiety driven by worry that their competitors "don't take days off," and so on.

Fortunately, the world of sport performance has placed more focus on the value of sleep and recovery over the last several years. Prior to that, it was difficult to convince an athlete or a coach that a day off would be of value. Athletes now are more accepting of intentional time away from their sport to decompress. Sometimes a few days are all that's needed, and sometimes it can take much longer. All of the variables related to an athlete's developmental and competitive process play a role.

In a micro sense, recovery applies to the time in between points or in between shots. In the work setting, it is the time in between meetings or tasks, such as a physician going from patient to patient. Being intentional about taking a moment—whether it's a breath or a three-second visualization—will allow you to detach from the hamster wheel we all have a tendency to run on. Some athletes utilize precise routines in between points or shots, but the effectiveness depends on whether that routine facilitates micro recovery.

In the end, **make sure that self-care and self-regulation are always in play so the intensity of deliberate training and development is counterbalanced by intentional "breaks" that allow you to remain healthy, centered, and grounded.**

28

WHAT IF THEY CALLED YOU **A CHAIR?**

AN ATHLETE WILL TELL ME:

"The coach doesn't think I'm good enough."
"My teammates don't think I'm very good."
"People have an opinion about me . . ." as an athlete, as a leader, or whatever.

There could be any number of scenarios where someone is somehow invested in other people's opinions. My typical response is, "What do you believe about you?"

The athlete might acknowledge that they know they are better than the stated opinion. From that point, I use a lot of nonsensical examples:

"Do you believe you're human? Do you believe that's true about you?"

"Yeah, I know I'm a human."

"Okay. Well, if you know that's true about you, what if somebody said that you're a chair? What would you think about that?"

"I would think they're nuts because they don't really know me."

"Exactly. So, as it relates to your capacity as an athlete, as it relates to your leadership potential, as it relates to something that you know is valid and true about you—why would you allow somebody's contrary opinion to have any influence over what you know to be true about you?"

Letting the opinions of others define how we see ourselves is like listening to the poor soul who's babbling on the street corner. A person can say whatever they want, but you don't have to give another person's opinion any power. Particularly if you know it's not true for you.

How do you know what's true? Sometimes it's a matter of redefining "good" or "bad" by getting down to the facts. Are you competent or capable? Do you have historical evidence to support your perception of competency?

If a coach is saying that they believe you're not qualified to be in the starting lineup for whatever reason, that is their opinion and you can respect their decision. This doesn't mean you have to agree with or argue against their perception. Their opinion about your role on a team is independent from what is factually accurate about your ability to potentially be successful in your task, and their reasons for not inserting you into the starting lineup may have little to do with your competency. There are a number of reasons why a coach may choose the lineup they choose.

There are a number of reasons why an opponent, a team member, a fan, or the media might have negative or contrary things to say about you as a person or as an athlete. **As it relates to your competency, it's up to you to gather evidence to support the facts and establish an objective reality.**

Once that's in place, another person's opinion about it is reasonable to consider, but in the end, it may be completely irrelevant. Don't give their opinion that power. Make sure that your honest accounting of yourself drives your opinion and is given the most weight.

29

THINK ABOUT AN ELEPHANT

PEOPLE FREQUENTLY ASK ME, "HOW DO I GET NEGATIVE thoughts out of my head?" Let's say a golfer is standing on the tee box, and he sees the water out there. All he can think about is hitting the ball into the water. We've all been there, so what's the answer? Don't think about the water? That can be difficult.

Fill your mind with something else that minimizes the power you were giving to the water. For example, if I were to say to you, "Whatever you do, I don't want you to think about an elephant." How are you going to pull that off? But if I were to say, while you're thinking about an elephant, "Okay, I want you to think about a giraffe—imagine its spots, its long neck, its ears flicking as it's munching on grass." Fill your mind with the vivid details of something else, and the elephant fades away.

Telling yourself to not think about something actually prompts the thought and gives it power. We want to give attention to what you want, so we start by filling your mind or fixing your attention on something else that is more productive than whatever you're trying to avoid. In the example of the golfer, I would want them to gently reattach to the target that they want to hit and spend an extra moment with that target or picture of the target being hit in their mind. The more there is clarity of intention of the shot they want to hit, the less energy is directed to trying to avoid the trouble.

Thoughts will get stuck in your head. Say you're a middle-distance runner who is on the start line and all you can think about is failing... or getting tripped. How do you get those thoughts out of your head? You don't. You regulate your internal environment by recognizing that this is an unproductive thought and then filling your head with more productive thoughts, choosing to be present within your body.

What we're really talking about is conscious competency around repetitive behavior or thought tendencies. I want to make sure that people have a heightened awareness of what they're doing, when they're doing it, and why they're doing it. There's no need to overthink it. With a higher level of awareness, we can be repetitive when we want to be repetitive, and we can flex or make adaptations if things aren't going the way we'd like them to go.

30

ACCEPT YOUR ROLE

ONE OF THE GREATEST CHALLENGES FOR ATHLETES IS TO accept the role they have been ascribed. It's useful to come to some level of acceptance with regard to where you are in relation to your teammates, the other competitors, or whoever is on the podium. Sometimes it's just true that on that day, another athlete was better than you. Or it may be true that some athletes are going to beat you.

I worked with multiple tennis pros who made it into the top 10 in the world and yet they never won a Grand Slam. Why? Because Serena Williams, Rafael Nadal, Roger Federer, and Novak Djokovic were dominating the world stage at that time. Anybody else who came along might be really good, but they were not good enough yet!

Note that I'm not suggesting that you be satisfied, simply that you have a level of acceptance for the reality you find yourself in. There is an important difference between being accepting and being satisfied. I like for athletes to always work toward being accepting and rarely allowing themselves to be satisfied. The reality might be that you weren't good enough today to win, or maybe the role ascribed to you by your coach is limited, different from what you might prefer. Whatever the case, if you thrash about internally, wishing it were different, or judging the way that it is without some sort of solution or actionable item, how will you be able to make an improvement?

Accept where you are today and, at the same time, know what you want to do to improve yourself—you don't have to be satisfied. You might think, *I'm going to go get stronger, and this is how I'm going to do it.* Even so, the **acceptance of your role in the moment can help you manage your immediate internal environment in a way that is more productive.**

When you accept your role, you effectively help flip the switch from *me vs. them* to *me vs. the task at hand.*

31

HOW DO YOU AFFECT YOUR **ENVIRONMENT?**

AMONG THE MANY LIFE (AND SPORT) LESSONS I LEARNED VIA Tim Elmore's Growing Leaders curriculum are a couple that use everyday metaphors to help us reflect on what you contribute to your environment. These concepts can be particularly useful in team and group settings.

We all have the opportunity to choose our attitude in any circumstance. Often, our mood and attitude will affect the people around us. A simple way to conceptualize this impact is to consider whether you function as a faucet or a drain.

When you are in your sport or work environment, is your attitude and energy something that is positively and constructively additive to the situation (i.e., a *faucet*), or would it be more accurate to describe your influence as a *drain*? This self-examination can be an enlightening and sometimes painful experience to undertake.

One of the most valuable assets that you can bring to your life experiences is to be additive, useful, and helpful to others. Being deeply honest with yourself about your "energy contributions" can go a long way toward assisting you in consistently working toward being a "faucet," facilitating success for yourself and for those on your "team," be it family members, teammates, co-workers, or peers.

Another way to consider how you influence your environment is by using the metaphor of whether you are a thermometer or a thermostat. A *thermometer* measures the temperature in the room. Knowing this information is beneficial, and a person who can go into a group situation and measure and read accurately what is happening in that situation can be of some value.

The *thermostat*, however, can impact the temperature in the room by raising or lowering it so that the temperature is optimal for that immediate situation. People who are capable and willing to act like a thermostat are highly influential in their group settings. The best coaches, team members, and staff members are the ones who can gauge accurately what's going on in a particular moment and be effective at adjusting the energy in the room to meet the needs of the circumstance.

This entails knowing when to bring energy, enthusiasm, or positivity to a situation where they are sensing low energy, complacency, or negativity. Conversely, they know how to use calmness, quiet, or silence to diffuse situations that are too "hot," stressful, or intense. This can be done verbally, with body language, or through eye contact.

Everyone has the capacity to operate more like a faucet and more like a thermostat. This is another one of the personal characteristics and intentional choices we can make in our life. While it may be true that this shift is easier or more natural or comfortable for some, that does not justify a lack of effort on the part of those who default to "drain" or "thermometer" mode. "I'm not wired that way" or "It's too hard for me to do that" are not acceptable excuses to shirk responsibility for attempting to be your best for the group.

Doing the intentional work to improve these skills gives you an opportunity to build a strength that can productively influence any subsequent collective setting in which you find yourself in your personal or professional life.

32

MAKE SURE THE LAST THING YOU DO IS **POSITIVE**

LET'S SAY A TENNIS PLAYER HITS A FOREHAND AND IT GOES in the net. At times, you'll see him repeat the motion, like a dry rep. He's simulating making the same mistake again without the ball.

Most people, in my experience, have a tendency to emotionalize and replay their mistakes, as opposed to their successes. This practice of rehearsing and reinforcing also applies to the rest of life.

At the end of a meeting, very rarely will a CEO say, "Man, I crushed it! I could tell the room was really buzzing when I said this, and they really got it when I did this." It's far more likely that they'll lament, "I really made a mistake with how I handled that, and I'm not sure people really understood slide four."

Our brains are hardwired to acknowledge threat potential. We are constantly looking for things that aren't going well, scanning our environment and storing in our brains the things that don't go well, the things we think might be painful—or even threatening. Those are the things that are most easily accessed in our memories because they're literally closer to the surface and more readily recalled. Unless it's truly an over-the-top experience—"Everybody was giving me a standing ovation afterward!"—we have a tendency to "bank" our moments of perceived inadequacy. If we're talking about an everyday business meeting, or some conversation you had, you won't typically come away from it reminding yourself what a good job you did; you'll be thinking about what you *didn't* do very well.

If you're going to do something post-execution, make sure you're either rehearsing an adjustment or reinforcing what you just did well. So, for some golfers, what works after hitting a shot they really liked is to swing the club again and get that same feel. Alternately, if they swing the club and hit a shot they don't like, rather than just throwing the club in the bag, they take a swing that feels good. *Then* they put the club in the bag.

Many athletes will be kinesthetically aware. They hit the shot, and they know their hips fired too early, so they rehearse it again and get a good swing where they can feel their hips doing what they want to do on the next swing. The same goes for the rehearsal swing pre-execution. You're still working to be sure that last one felt good. If there is an adjustment to be made next time you execute your task, mentally rehearse and reinforce the adjustment in a way that is productive. This decreases the likelihood that you will be lying in bed at night wishing you "hadn't said or done it that way." This is where people start getting into rumination and perseveration. It will be easier to get to sleep if instead you are reminding yourself of what you've done well and have clarity about your adjustment for next time!

33

HONESTLY AND ACCURATELY **EVALUATE YOURSELF**

EVERY ATHLETE IS LOOKING FOR A BLUEPRINT FOR SUCCESS— what to work on, how to get better at whatever they're doing. There are also times when some athletes are disinclined to take in subjective feedback or objective data. It's almost like they don't want to hear those sorts of things. Maybe they don't trust input from certain people. Admittedly, I wouldn't want athletes to trust *everybody's* input, because obviously, some people aren't qualified to give it. But it's imperative that people be willing to take in as much objective and factual input as possible. This gives them a baseline or point of reference so they can then make improvements.

The easy feedback is obviously the tangibly measurable type that comes from the time on a stopwatch or the weight on a barbell, showing that you are in fact jumping higher, running faster, getting stronger. But beyond that are the mental-emotional aspects of performance. Things like how well you are composing yourself in training or in practice or how well sustained is your focus. There are a number of variables or metrics that can be woven into the equation that express your development and success as an athlete. And **it's important that you remain receptive to that feedback and**

input—whether it's coming from others, the data, video, or whatever else—and weigh the accuracy of it.

Here's an example. In golf, when I'm doing online sessions, I'm beholden to the athlete's perception of how they played, because I didn't actually watch them play. Post-competition, I will ask, "How did it go?" And I will regularly hear, "I was hitting the ball so well when I was warming up before the round on the range, and then I got on the golf course and I didn't hit it very well."

There are certainly times where there are issues with transferability of practice or a warm-up session into the competitive arena. Other times I'll ask the coach what they observed: "How was Amy's warm-up on the range?" Without hesitation, the coach might say, "Oh, geez, she was hitting it all over the place."

In my own observation of athletes like Amy, this discrepancy plays out something like this: I'll watch her hit several poor-quality drivers, and then all of a sudden, she starts hitting it well on the range. She then puts the driver away and goes to the course and plays erratically. So, in response to the comment, "I was hitting it so well on the range," my take is, "Okay, yeah, shots 8, 9, and 10 were pretty good. But 1 through 7 were not very consistent."

Some people are super hard on themselves. No matter what they do, there's self-judgment that impairs their ability to give themselves accurate feedback. And then there are other people who are borderline delusional, occupying the other end of the spectrum where they're selective in what they remember about how they prepared or trained or played. That lack of objectivity or receptivity can lead to real challenges and keep them from putting their energy into developing areas of real promise and opportunity. Where might you fall on that spectrum?

34

ACCEPTANCE VS. SATISFACTION

WHEN I TALK ON THE CONCEPT OF ACCEPTANCE, I OCCASIONALLY get pushback from a coach or an athlete about their interpretation of this word. This is another occasion for precise language and making sure everyone is on the same page. The resistance I receive often revolves around the athlete saying they can't accept anything less than what they ultimately want because they don't ever want to be satisfied. In their way of interpreting this, *acceptance* loosely translates into being satisfied with where they are at, and thus this creates a concern about continued motivation and effort.

I propose to all with whom I consult that they work feverishly to accept whatever is real and factually accurate about a situation. (The trite phrase "It is what it is" fits well here.) Additionally, I align with the athlete by saying I agree that I always want them to be slightly dissatisfied with where they are, as long as this generates fuel for them to continue to work on their growth and development. This is how we land on this statement: **Accept everything and be fully satisfied with nothing.**

Working toward acceptance before and after a situation helps minimize judgment, and not being fully satisfied with anything keeps fire in your belly. This is exactly the internal environment in which I'd like my clients to be.

35

REACTION VS. RESPONSE

THESE TWO WORDS ARE OFTEN USED INTERCHANGEABLY, and arguably they generally mean the same thing. I frequently differentiate between reaction and response, which seems to resonate with athletes and coaches.

I see a *reaction* as something that is reflexive and nearly instantaneous. The reaction happens almost simultaneously with some sort of activating event. A poor shot is hit, an easy catch is dropped, an amazing moment is realized, or something else happens that triggers an immediate internal and/or external result. The *response*, however, is the more conscious choice to subsequently regulate one's thoughts and behaviors in order to move past whatever has just occurred.

Often, coaches and athletes and parents and business executives get caught up in getting people to moderate their reactions and avoid extremes. This makes sense to a degree, as we don't want people reacting in a way that is inappropriate or breaches the cultural norms of whatever environment they find themselves in. Throwing golf clubs, slamming tennis rackets on the ground, screaming at a business associate—these behaviors are unhealthy and unacceptable. On the other hand, I think a certain amount of grace can be given to a momentary and reasonably subdued reaction when someone expresses temporary frustration, anger, excitement, or disbelief.

In my opinion, the real objective is to not let the instantaneous reaction influence your internal environment for any longer than a couple of seconds. This is when you commit to the challenging work of responding with optimal self-talk and being deliberate with body language. **We want the response to be intelligent and intentional so that the net effect can be beneficial.**

One example could be after winning a very difficult tennis point, a player might *react* with internal self-talk that emphasizes their likelihood of winning (future-oriented and outcome-based): "Oh my gosh, I'm going to beat this guy finally." I would want him to *respond* by redirecting his internal dialogue to be more present and task-oriented: "Hey, stay focused on this point and continue to attack his backhand. There's a lot more match to play."

On the other side of the coin, if a basketball player misses a free throw and then commits a turnover on the next possession, she might initially *react* with body language that conveys her disgust—her eyes downcast, shaking her head. In a subsequent time-out I would want her to *respond* by picking up her pace to get to the bench, keeping her eyes on or above the horizon.

- What sorts of internal and external reactions have you discovered are habits for you?
- How well do you mitigate or minimize those reactionary moments?
- How can you be more intentional in your response strategies?

Allowing some latitude for moderate reactions and putting emphasis on personal accountability for subsequent responses can go a long way toward building a solid foundation of mental discipline.

36

WHERE'S THE FIRE EXTINGUISHER?

THE SCIENCE SUPPORTING THE BENEFITS OF USING IMAGERY and visualization is compelling. Imagery has the potential to stimulate the brain, reduce physical and emotional stress, evoke emotions, and impact physiological reactions to assist in management of anxiety and depression. It can also help with the reduction of pain.

One of the ways that I utilize imagery with my clients is by having them visualize or imagine themselves in a multitude of challenging or less-than-preferred situations related to training or competing. It's not that I want them to conjure up a variety of "nightmare scenarios," but I do want them to mentally work through the adaptations and adjustments they might make in such circumstances. Here's the prompt: "If a metaphorical fire starts, what type of fire extinguisher might you access and use?" Many athletes are initially afraid of any number of plausible scenarios—it's the "what-ifs" and imagined situations that rattle them. My response is simple: "So what if that happens—what are some options available to you?"

A small contingent of my clients will initially resist the notion of allowing themselves to even imagine a less-than-desirable scenario. They worry that they will be "jinxing themselves if they think it" or "giving life to it," thus making its occurrence more likely. Ultimately,

I will respect the client's right to reject or modify anything I'm proposing, but first I ask them to consider how much better and secure it typically feels to be prepared in the event of an emergency.

Let's say you get a flat tire on the race course. See yourself managing that emotionally well. See yourself going through the motions of changing the tire as quickly as possible. This can apply to whatever adversity the athlete might encounter. Obviously, one can't imagine every possible permutation of things that could go wrong in competition. And I don't want people to have nonpreferred scenarios bouncing around in their heads for too long. But it's helpful to make a plan to address things that could reasonably happen—you got the start time wrong so now you have to shorten your warm-up. How do you deal with that?

In other words, if a fire starts, I want you to know where the fire extinguisher is, and I want you to know how to use it. **While I don't want you thinking about fires all the time, I do want you to realize, *Hey, I'm capable of overcoming adversity. Here's how I would manage that situation.***

Taking this a step further, sometimes I ask athletes to think of a scenario outside of their sport that serves as evidence of their strength and capacity for coping. Every one of us has overcome adversity. Every one of us has had a challenge that we figured out how to manage. As it's been said, "You've overcome 100 percent of your bad days." After all, you are still here to talk about it. I'm constantly pointing people to leverage their capacity to overcome things. So, what are some of those things for you? What are some of your coping strategies? First, tease out what has worked well for you, then take that and apply it to a specific scenario in your sport and life.

Many athletes, even doubters, end up being appreciative and excited about the payoff of having done the preliminary work of seeing themselves overcome adverse situations. I have repeatedly been told that when an unexpected situation plays out, proactive mental reps contribute to a sense of calm and action rather than a response of panic, confusion, or "paralysis."

Do the mental training work to create some situations in your mind, see yourself responding to them intelligently and productively, and be prepared to appreciate the benefits when you respond productively to something unfortunate.

Build internal acceptance for the possibility that shit might happen. If it does, you will be ready to handle it.

37

EFFECTIVE COMMUNICATION

COMMUNICATION IS INTEGRAL TO THE PRACTICE OF BECOMING One Day Better. On the surface, this idea seems so obvious and fundamental. The more an athlete can engage with her entire system around her as it relates to her sport development, sport performance, and sport experience, the more she can expect to grow and develop.

Effective feedback is openly and vulnerably communicated in a safe, trustworthy environment by trustworthy people. This is often the challenging part of getting feedback from others because not only does it take time to cultivate trust, but it helps to have everyone in the athlete's "bubble" in alignment.

Communication efficiencies (and breakdowns) can be quite apparent in observing doubles partners, whether in beach volleyball, tennis, or pickleball. Here is what I'm paying attention to:

- Are the athletes interacting in a way that is productive for both of them?
- Are they listening?
- Are they communicating effectively?
- Are they willing to receive input? And are they willing to receive input in the moment, even if it's stressful?

- Are they willing to be ready to adapt and flex through communication with the people around them, to minimize tension or confusion within their "bubble" of support?

I worked with professional doubles pickleball players who were having some challenges reading each other's body language and were communicating in unproductive ways. For example, one person was hesitant to say something because they were afraid their partner might take it in a particular way. There was also some conflict around tactical decisions. In between points, they were arguing about what sort of tactic to employ in the next point.

I didn't have to be physically present to observe these breakdowns in communication. I watched a match online, and as soon as the point was over (it didn't go very well), the athlete turned her back on her partner and walked away.

We want contact between points, touching paddles, eyes on one another—we want communication. If you turn your back and walk away, I don't know how to read that as your partner. *Are you mad at yourself? Are you disengaging to get your focus back? Are you angry with me?* And now there's this metacognition where I'm overly aware of what I'm thinking and what my partner is thinking, or I'm thinking about my own thinking—all of which takes me out of player mode.

When the mixed doubles pickleball players improved their communication, they manifested their physical potential on the court and ranked in the top 10 teams in the world. It took some time and a tolerance for tension, but tension acknowledged can be less intimidating than leaving it unspoken.

There's an ebb and flow to determining with a partner, with a teammate, with a coach, or whoever, what is the most effective way to communicate. It's a challenge within a team because obviously, everybody has their own preferred style or tolerance. A coach is not going to change their communication in a group setting to match the nuances of 17 different people's preferences. But it's important to understand, particularly in a group setting, that a lot of times, there's a lot that's missed because people receive information in a variety of different ways and communicate in ways that are sometimes quite different from one another. It can be uncomfortable.

On a daily basis I talk with athletes about issues specific to communication. Ultimately, there is no one right way to communicate; it's about finding the most effective, productive way.

Athletes will ask me, "Do I really have to do that?"

I always respond, "No, only if you want to win."

38

FOCUS ON **THE PROCESS,** NOT ON THE OUTCOME

COUNTLESS BOOKS AND PODCASTS FOCUS ON PROCESS VERSUS outcome. Part of the reason why topics like this are cliché is because they are deeply rooted in truth. Admittedly, this is the No. 1 mental practice I deal with in my work with athletes—glaring examples of outcome orientation, and its subtle nuances as well. It's often seen in an athlete who is so focused on whether they're going to win or lose in a moment that the athlete loses focus due to being overly excited or overly worried. This manifests at times in forgetting to "do their job" in that moment. Sometimes you miss things that you would normally see. Sometimes you tighten up and lose the free flow and flexibility that you trained your body to produce in those moments.

People are largely unaware of how they allow their thought processes to be influenced by even the slightest hint of outcome or consequence relative to results. This can distract them from being present and process-oriented, focused on doing their task in the moment. It's important to make a distinction between awareness and attention. **Being aware of the outcome is not a problem. But how much attention do you give it?**

Oftentimes people give *attention* to the outcome, and that draws their attention away from the process. When I tell an athlete to focus on *process*, I mean for them to engage with deep focus in the task they are in, rather than putting their energy toward a result—or the consequence of a result.

In 90 percent of the conversations I have, there's something that rubs up against the effect that people allow an outcome to have on themselves, whether it's in a moment or connected to a longer-term outcome, such as:

Am I going to make the starting lineup?
Am I going to be able to earn a living?
Am I going to get drafted?
Am I going to make the Olympic team?

There are subtle daily outcome hits. And then there are also bigger-picture outcome hits that can drag you away from the process at hand.

It's more of a push than a pull strategy if you bring a One Day Better approach. *Where am I now, and is it pushing me in a direction—as opposed to pulling me toward an outcome?* Again, the distinction between awareness and attention is critical here.

Being aware of the outcome, one desires to stay on track. Sure, having that North Star or dream can be helpful, productive, and even inspiring. It can keep you generally on course. But now shift your attention back to the present: *What do I do right now to be One Day Better? How do I develop and improve whatever my skill is and however I aim to progress?* Whatever that variable is, is it pushing me in the direction of mastery in that skill?

39

FOCUS ON **EFFORT**

AMONG THE GREAT CHALLENGES FOR ATHLETES AND COACHES is that they often fixate on things over which they have little or no control. Coaches want to control what the athletes are doing and thinking, athletes want to control the coaches' opinions or decisions, and each of them wants to control any number of things they might be able to influence but over which they do not have full control.

I put a lot of emphasis on the person taking full advantage of the moment/situation by making sure the athlete/coach is directing their energy largely toward their controllable inputs rather than getting distracted by their real or imagined output. Of course, I want everyone to take information from their outputs so that they can make intelligent adjustments and adaptations. If something you're doing isn't working in a moment, acknowledging that with a proposed adjustment makes sense:

"I'm impulsively swinging at curveballs."
"My cross-court forehand is hitting the ball long."
"My serves are erratic."

On the other hand, I want to make sure that they are accurately assessing how much effort they are putting in at any particular moment.

Regularly, I hear athletes lamenting the fact that they didn't get the result they wanted, only to later look back with objectivity and admit that their effort at some point dropped—whether it was their mental or physical effort. Doing an honest and objective assessment of one's effort can be very difficult at times. Often it is not until after a situation that we realize we weren't really, truly "all in" with our exertion.

I want athletes and coaches to do routine check-ins to make sure they are giving all they have to give in a particular situation. Often, they are not—they might be pacing themselves, distracted by a previous circumstance or worried about a moment to come.

One of the success criteria I propose for athletes and coaches is that they literally grade themselves on their effort and incorporate ways in future circumstances to continually push their effort needle to be as close to 100 percent as possible. Maybe you didn't get the outcome you wanted, but did you max the effort? Or did you achieve the desired result, but you had more in your tank than you thought? In that case, it's a less painful disappointment.

Effort is one of the extremely small number of things over which we have complete control. Direct your attention toward your effort, and you've significantly increased your likelihood for success—and additionally, you've increased your likelihood for enjoyment as well.

40

GET TO, NOT HAVE TO

FREEDOM IS A WONDERFUL IDEA. HOWEVER, IF YOU REALLY want to become better or achieve something meaningful, you will surrender some freedom in the process. In committing to any big goal, you narrow the choices that you can reasonably make while still giving yourself a chance to achieve that goal. This can and will impose limits on how you spend your time, but it also affects myriad aspects of daily life. If you want to be a world-class athlete, what you will do at the gym or how you will approach sleep and nutrition have just become vastly restricted.

Narrowing your choices gives you the greatest possibility for success. And there will be times when it puts your desire to the test. If your motivation wanes, you might find yourself in situations where your behavior is not aligned with where you want to go. Attention to your craft is easily compromised when there are other things you want to do or freedoms you want to exercise.

What we are really talking about is the dissonance between who you say you want to be and what you are doing. Line up your behavior with your intention by narrowing the choices. It's not about setting absolutes or ultimatums. Instead, become conscious of the choices you make and why you are making them.

In light of this awareness, notice when you are using "have to" language. Athletes will tell me about how they "have to" get up early tomorrow to lift weights, or that they "have to" practice until dinnertime, or how they "have to" travel all weekend for their competitions.

It is important for athletes to change this self-talk to "get to" language. What's real is that you get to train, practice, and/or compete. You are choosing this intentionally, because you have long-term interests in your preparation, development, and competitive endeavors.

I appreciate that given the opportunity to get up at 5 a.m. to go to the gym or to sleep for a while longer, you might, in the moment, wish to sleep as opposed to getting up early to exercise. However, if you put your attention on your long-term interests and your long-term goals, you will realize that while in the short term you might immediately prefer to sleep longer or do something other than train or travel, **you are choosing to work, train, and compete because your ultimate ambitions are greater than your immediate preferences.**

You don't *have to* do the work to be great—you *choose to* and thus you *get to*!

Savor these choices as an opportunity to engage more deeply with what you are striving to achieve and who you are striving to become. Undisciplined choices made in the moment can add up and inhibit the likelihood of achieving greatness.

Make sure what you want most is given priority over what you want in the *moment*.

41

THERE'S ONLY ONE GAME OR POINT THAT'S **RELEVANT**

ONE OF THE MOST ENJOYABLE TASKS I GET TO DO WITH SEVERAL of the teams/athletes with whom I work is team-building sessions or retreats. These events usually occur at the beginning of the year when the new team is getting to know one another and create their own set of rules, cultural norms, and intentions for the season ahead. I also look for timely opportunities to introduce One Day Better concepts.

If the team goes on a long hike or hill/mountain climb, I will ask, "Which step in this hike is the most relevant?" This generally elicits some input and debate:

> "The first one—without it, nothing happens."
> "The last one because the journey's not over until you finish it."
> "The most challenging moments are when the ground is slippery or steep or difficult to navigate."

It's my own philosophy that while all of the steps are important, there is actually only one step that is relevant—the one you find yourself in at any particular moment.

It's common for coaches, athletes, media, or anyone in the realm of sports to place more significance on certain moments in the competition or specific times in the season. Here are some familiar refrains:

In baseball or softball: "The first inning is crucial."
In tennis: "Tiebreakers are most important."
More generally, "Once the conference games start, it's time to take it up a notch."
"Post-season is when it really counts."

These interpretations create an internal environment that switches on or off based on the perceived level of importance. Finding themselves in a situation that carries increased significance, athletes often attempt to do more, be more, try harder—which rarely generates the desired performance. On the other side of the coin, some athletes allow their intensity or intention to become diffused and/or compromised because it is "just the regular season" or "early in the contest."

My remedy: **Train yourself to approach every point as the most relevant point when you're in it. When you are no longer in it, consider it irrelevant.** Two games from now against that opponent is important but not relevant until you prepare for and play them—focus on this next game first. That missed opportunity in the last few minutes means nothing as it relates to taking care of the task in front of you now.

The "best of the best" work diligently to treat every rep of every workout and every moment of every competition with the same high value. Of course, this is difficult to do, but that is ultimately what we are striving for—to see that the most relevant moment is the one you are in—so get all you can out of this moment, right here, right now.

42

ELIMINATE ADJECTIVES FOR **TRAINING AND COMPETITION**

I AM A FANATIC ABOUT WORD USAGE BECAUSE OF THE IMPACT of certain words. Using precise language can positively impact and influence your mental state and attitude. And on the other side of the coin, using imprecise language can negatively influence your internal environment.

Seemingly benign and ordinary language generates a slightly skewed thought process for many individuals. For this reason, I recommend minimizing, if not eliminating, adjectives in connection with training or competition. A "big" contest, a situation in a game that is "crucial," or a training session that is "important" can signal to the athlete that there is either more on the line and/or the situation requires they do more, work harder, or be more intense. It is clearly true that some situations are more consequential than others and these sorts of adjectives seem more "accurate." While I can appreciate that adjectives like these can potentially be beneficial in directing one's focus or engagement, I like my clients to recognize how these types of words can influence how they focus and engage in the moment. Consider some examples:

- "tough" opponents vs. "weak" opponents
- "hard" situations vs. "easy" situations
- "critical" moments vs. "ordinary" moments

Many athletes inadvertently allow their focus and intensity to fluctuate based on how they perceive the situation. The best athletes address any number of different situations as similarly as possible. I want athletes to work to optimally engage, achieve focus, and bring a level of intensity to *every* situation, not just the ones they perceive to matter more. Too many adjectives and labels create a yo-yo effect for the athlete's internal environment. By labeling the situation factually and objectively, it's possible to establish an internal equilibrium:

- an "easy" opponent becomes simply Team "X"
- a "difficult" race becomes a 5K race
- a "tough" golf hole becomes a 435-yard par 4 that doglegs to the right

Minimize labels and adjectives to help mitigate the ups and downs of stress, worry, and focus.

Next time you listen to sports announcers call a game or contest, listen for the constant flow of adjectives describing how "crucial," "important," "life-changing," or "stressful" the situation is. It's a useful model of what is unlikely to work well in your own head. If you want to think like a champion, use precise language to steady your internal environment.

43

IF YOU DON'T FEEL IT, ACT LIKE IT

I HAVE NEVER BEEN A FAN OF "FAKE IT TILL YOU MAKE IT." The intention in such a directive is for people to exude the confidence, belief, and competencies they may not actually be experiencing. There may be constructive value in this idea in some instances, but the word "fake" seems to sanction being inauthentic and phony, rather than authentic and real. "Impostor syndrome" is a significant challenge for many people, and I suspect that being instructed to fake it can further contribute to this perception. I propose this subtle change in wording: **Despite the fact that you might not *feel* a particular way, you can act in ways to increase your odds of overriding that feeling.**

As an example, I am constantly encouraging my clients to act with courage and act with bravery even though they are scared, nervous, or underconfident. By engaging the physical actions that align with what you want to elicit, you aren't faking it. Rather, you are doing the necessary things that create change even though you may not "feel it" yet.

You can exhibit courageous body language by standing upright, fixing your eyes above the horizon, and unclenching your fists even though you might be feeling angry or down or discouraged. There is solid research to support the idea that behaving "as if" you feel differently has a significant impact within your body. From a hormonal, biochemical, and physiological perspective, actions like smiling, slowing down your movements, shifting your eyes upward, and uncrossing your arms can send signals to your body that things are "okay."

The next time you're not feeling how you'd like to feel in a particular moment, change your behavior, body language, or actions to give yourself a chance to more quickly recover to a healthier internal space of increased confidence and belief.

44

"HIRE" A CONSTRUCTIVE COACH

I AM A FIRM BELIEVER THAT THE MOST IMPORTANT COACH IN the life of an athlete is the one who lives in their own head. In your commitment to performance, you are continuously engaged in a routine of assessing things and generating input and feedback to improve the process or outcome. You would be hard-pressed to find a coach who knows you and your history better than you do.

Evaluate the quality and effectiveness of the coach in your head:

- Is the way you are wording things helpful and constructive?
- Would you say the same things to someone you are guiding or teaching that you're saying to yourself?
- How do you coach yourself after mistakes are made? How encouraging are you? Are you overly tolerant of excuses, do you allow too much wiggle room, or is it more the case that you are a perfectionist, unable to accept any slipups or errors?

While it is extremely valuable for most athletes to have outside coaching input from people who are experts at skill, physical, and/or tactical development, it is also valuable for the athlete to honor and respect their internal coach. **Ensure that this voice is constructive rather than judgmental, is honest and fair, and communicates in an effective way.**

This work is well worth your energy as you progress toward a goal. After all, this is one of the few things within your control—how you choose to speak to yourself.

45

CHART YOUR PROGRESS

ONE OF THE MOST EFFECTIVE WAYS TO GAUGE, MEASURE, AND evaluate the success of your developmental process is to consistently gather information and data from which to make an honest assessment. Today, there are innumerable variations of tracking devices and apps to capture physiological, statistical, tactical, and self-reported data. Prior to this proliferation of technology, much of this information had to be captured, stored, and interpreted by the athlete and/or their coach.

I vividly remember my first session with a professional hockey player who would later skate his way into the NHL Hall of Fame. He showed up to my office with a large duffel bag. After our introduction, he unzipped the bag to show me the dozens of journals wherein he had painstakingly written his daily goals, daily feedback, and any other random or applicable thoughts or feelings or lessons learned. There were literally thousands of pages of notes he'd taken, spanning from the time he was a young boy on the ice up through his fourth year in the NHL when he'd sought me out. He is an extreme example of someone who took seriously the notion that tracking his progress would give him information that would support his confidence—giving clear evidence of the reps he'd experienced. Additionally, he used the information to help guide him in what adjustments to make and what to continue doing.

I've witnessed hundreds of elite athletes who take the time to employ a daily journal, write in a diary, keep a logbook, or make notes in their phone. The benefits of the developmental clarity that flows from this practice has been proven again and again.

Take the time to chart your progress. You will more clearly see where you've been, where you are in this moment, and where you're heading.

46

TELL YOURSELF **WHAT YOU WANT** TO HAVE HAPPEN

IT'S ALL TOO COMMON FOR ATHLETES AND COACHES TO CONTACT me and start out by telling me about what they don't want to happen. In truth, this is how a lot of people approach sport, trying to avoid a negative. Maybe they are trying not to strike out, trying not to bonk, trying not to lose their roster spot.

One of the simplest mental tips I offer is guidance toward imagery and language. Tell me what you *do* want to have happen rather than what you're trying to avoid. **Reframe your perspective in terms of desired outcomes or desired training.**

When we're operating in avoidance mode, many of us are truly unaware of how to use language or imagery. Here's an example of how this conversation plays out in golf when I ask a golfer to tell me what her swing thoughts are.

"Well, you know, I'm really trying to not take the club outside. I don't want to come across the line because when I do, then I get this big slice."

"Okay, so you're trying to not take it outside and you're trying to not have the club go across the line, so you don't get that sort of a shot shape?"

"Yeah, exactly."

"Okay, well, what *are* you trying to do?"

After a long pause, she states, "I guess what I'm trying to do is have the club come down the line, so it stays on plane—so the ball comes out this way and I get a different shot."

Now we have a visual plan and specific language for what we want to have happen. Athletes will often tell me, "I rarely think about it that way."

Avoidance behavior is so common, not only in sports, but in life. How many people are trying to not fail the test or trying to not make people upset? As humans, we are often hardwired to avoid a threat, so we go through life trying not to screw up. Approaching any situation in this way has the potential to inhibit you from giving yourself an opportunity to go get what you want.

"I'm trying not to be overweight." Do you want to be healthy? Do you want to be fit? Do you see yourself as someone who prioritizes good nutrition? What's the picture or specific outcome you want?

This is simple stuff, but it's hard to employ. What we're really talking about is overriding current habits and building new habits. It's easy to careen through life just doing our own thing, unaware of what we're doing to ourselves. Maybe you have a habit of constantly thinking about how to avoid negative events you're making up in your own head—threats that might not even be real. It's just that you're thinking in a particular way, telling yourself what you need to do, and now you are stressed and anxious. It's hard to break the habit of avoidance, but the concept itself is simple. Redirect your thoughts and language to what you desire.

47

YOUR THOUGHTS MAKE YOU MAD

WHEN I FIRST CONSULT WITH A CLIENT, ONE OF THE FIRST models we discuss is the idea that thoughts influence feelings, which influence behavior. The dynamic between these three things—thoughts, emotions, and actions—is at the center of mental discipline and training.

It's my belief that if you can understand how and when your thoughts are creating emotions that are not productive, you can be intentional about changing your thoughts, which can influence your emotions and then help guide more productive thoughts.

This is significant because it's human nature that we speak loosely around the idea that *situations* create our emotions:

"Being in the game makes me nervous."
"Talking to my coach makes me scared."
"Missing those shots makes me mad."
"Not executing well makes me frustrated."

In fact, none of these situations *makes* you feel any particular way. You choose to think about your situation in a particular way, and the thoughts create the emotion. As an example, I will ask golfers if they believe that missing a 3-foot putt makes them angry. Nearly all of them will say yes.

I will then ask, "Is it literally *every time* that you miss a 3-foot putt—in practice, on the putting green and slightly distracted while on the phone, or in a casual round with friends? Does each of these instances elicit anger?"

They then respond, "No, it depends on the situation."

So, it is not missing the putt that generates the emotion; it is a result of your perception of the situation's importance or value. The impact and benefits of deeply understanding this concept cannot be overemphasized. When a person begins to take ownership of their responses to situations, massive mental shifts can take place.

First, work to identify what you are feeling:

"I'm angry right now," or
"I'm feeling really nervous."

From here, you can start to reconstruct what your thoughts are that make you feel how you are feeling and choose different perspectives or ways to respond. This puts you in a position to be more in control of your emotions.

Make no mistake about it—people are going to naturally be frustrated or angry or nervous in certain situations. This is not about functioning without emotion. The true art is in reframing the emotion so it becomes useful or productive rather than destructive. It starts with an honest examination of what you are thinking and a willingness to adjust your thoughts.

The reality is that things that happened to you do not make you mad, do not make you angry, do not make you sad, and do not make you anxious. **What makes you mad are the thoughts you have around particular situations.** Consequently, if you can change your thoughts, you can influence your emotions.

> **The traffic jam** in front of you is not what makes you mad. It's the fact that you're thinking, *This shouldn't be here right now. I should be able to get there faster. How can it possibly be this slow?*

> **Anger** doesn't emanate from circumstances or situations. It stems from our interpretation of a circumstance or our thoughts about a situation. Ask yourself, *How am I choosing to think about this? How might I adjust the way I'm thinking to mitigate an emotion that's unproductive?*

Not all anger is unproductive, but take ownership of the fact that you're the one creating it for yourself. Then ask, *How is it helpful to have that emotion? Is there a different way to look at this?*

48

YOU CAN'T HAVE **EVERYTHING**

PEOPLE HAVE A FASCINATION WITH HOW THOSE WHO ARE AT the top of their industry achieved success. There have been hundreds of books written, examinations done, and studies undertaken regarding what characteristics or what methods impact those who are successful at their given craft. In nearly every situation in which I've been involved with these highest of achievers, one of the common denominators is having, at times, an "unbalanced" life that has been devoted to putting extraordinary intentional effort and time into their growth and development.

Thankfully, in the past decade or so, people have started to become more aware of the mental health implications in the upper echelons of sport performance. The "win at all costs" and "grind and sacrifice" notions of athlete development can carry plenty of ramifications when driven by obsession or compulsion over attaining gold medals or championships. Similarly, in the world of age-group endurance athletes alone there are innumerable examples of people whose attempt to be both the best in their work environment and the best in their sport environment takes a tragic toll on their job or their athletic life . . . or both.

This has led to a recent outcry about athlete development, allowing for a more balanced lifestyle as skills are acquired.

Certainly, I am a strong advocate of putting one's mental/emotional health as a priority above any sort of achievement. However, it remains true that mastery involves plenty of pushing, and the extent of the gray area between "balanced" and "unbalanced" is unique to every individual. Only through scrutiny and clear feedback can a determination be made about how much one can "unbalance" and still be healthy and productive.

It is naïve for people to believe they can live a "normal" balanced life and achieve at the highest levels. Here's my advice: **You can give yourself a chance to be great at anything you want, but not everything you want.** For the university student-athletes with whom I've consulted, to be the best of the best in sport means that either academics, social life, spiritual pursuits, or other needs are not going to get their full or optimal attention. I don't think that's bad or wrong. There's no judgment, but the fact remains: It is physically impossible to be your 100 percent best at everything.

Learning to accept that being in the upper echelons requires significant effort and demands deep investment in time and energy, and being willing to accept that other things will be underprioritized, is something for athletes or high performers to reconcile.

Monitor your mental, physical, and emotional health first, and accept that becoming great entails a willingness to do the work and put in the required effort. This means accepting stretches of time or seasons where life is definitively unbalanced.

49

THE ONLY FAILURE IS A FAILURE TO LEARN

GREAT ATHLETES—OLYMPIC MEDALISTS, WORLD CHAMPIONS, national champions, athletes who have risen to be the best in the world in their respective sports—know how to manage and respond to failure productively.

Every athlete who is invested in their craft is going to initially be upset with failure. No one likes to perform poorly, no one likes to lose. However, in time, the athletes with mental fortitude recognize that in every failure there is a lesson. There is something to learn every time you are practicing, training, or competing—even in those times when things don't go well. Many of the best athletes understand that failure is a necessary requirement if they are pushing themselves past their limits, seeking growth outside of their comfort zone, and/or simply getting the requisite reps and experience in order to be wiser/better/stronger as they develop.

The only real failure on the part of most athletes is when they fail to see the lesson inherent in the painful experience, and they fail to learn and apply the available lesson. When I am coaching or consulting with an athlete, I describe every rep, every experience, every day, as being a "+1" experience. What this means is that **even those situations that feel substandard or like a regression are not counted**

as a "-1" as long as you are aware of the lesson drawn from the failure and that lesson is applied. That failure is now additive to your development, as a "+1" day or experience.

This is the mentality of the very best athletes—even when they're not at their best. It is building a One Day Better habit of helpful application from every experience, whether it's a joyful or a painful one!

50

REGAIN CONCENTRATION ON THE **TASK AT HAND**

ONE OF THE PRIMARY CONSTRUCTS OF MENTAL TRAINING IS *attentional control.* Wherever it is that you find yourself—in the lead-up to a training session or during the training session, pre-competition or mid-competition—there's a natural tendency for your attention to wander. In sports psychology, this is known as *attentional drift.* Your attention drifts in a way that is basically outside of your awareness, and sometimes it can feel like it's outside of your control. In these moments, we want the athlete to regain attentional control with an intentional and purposeful attentional shift.

Athletes will frequently ask me, "Okay, so when my mind wanders, what do I do with it? How do I stop myself from being distracted?" The answer, as I prescribe it, is not about imposing a strict set of rules.

When you're aware that you're not focused on what you want to be focused on, try simply shifting your attention to the task that's right in front of you. It's often beneficial to simply reorient yourself to the present moment and the task at hand. **What's right in front of you? What is important right now?** If you were doing your job well in this moment, what would you be doing?

If you are in the middle of a pregame meal, this might mean you shift your attention to the taste of your food, the process of chewing, and the feeling of the chair you are sitting in. If you're in the middle of a competitive contest, the game is telling you what to put your attention on—there's something constructive right in front of you to which you can redirect your attention.

Every sport has its own set of relevant cues that can bring a person back to task. For example, if you are preparing to return a serve in tennis, it might be that one of your relevant cues is watching the toss of the ball to pick up early information about where the serve might go. If you're a volleyball player, you might be watching the approach angle of somebody attacking the net to get a sense of where the ball might be hit. These relevant cues can offer clues on what to do next from an action perspective. By consistently dragging your inattention back to these cues and sustaining your focus as long as possible, you are more likely to be in a good place to be able to execute.

To some extent, attentional drift is inevitable. Respond by shifting your attention to a relevant cue or whatever the task is that's right in front of you.

51

PRACTICE AS IF IT IS A **TOURNAMENT**

ONCE AN ATHLETE HAS THE REQUISITE SKILLS AND A LEVEL OF proficiency about how to do what they do, they can have a tendency to practice with less intensity. This can compromise the transferability of what they're doing now or cause them to fall short of what they want to be doing once they get into a competitive environment. For example, I'll watch a golfer play a practice round in advance of a tournament, and I will notice that they're not preparing as thoroughly or comprehensively before each shot as I know they are likely to do in a competition. The athlete takes shortcuts in assembling information about the shot that's in front of them. I have been known to ask, "If this shot were to win the US Open, would you have prepared the same way? Would you have prepared the same way if this was a moment of more significance to you?"

Inevitably, the athlete will respond that they probably would have been more intentional or would have taken more care to do whatever they do. It begs the question, "So why are you shortcutting?"

Make your habits of preparation as transferable as possible to the competitive arena. The notion that you're going to simply "flip a switch" when the tournament comes or when the competition starts is deeply flawed.

If an athlete hasn't built repetition in practice and formed habits around their preparation, they're unlikely to elicit that on a consistent basis in competition. In fact, I would argue that they're probably greatly inhibited from eliciting those sorts of quality habits in some respects because once athletes are under stress, they sort of "forget" what to do. If they haven't built skills and habits that are more automated, they often leave pieces of their preparation out during tournament play or in competition.

Once a certain level of skill has been acquired, it's time to dial in your preparation. Skill acquisition is an important caveat because in early skill acquisition, there will be times where you will benefit by just working on technique or some tactical adjustment. But when those things are done, you enter into the pre-competition phase. Now you want to do the things that replicate the competition as much as possible, to create transferability and overlap. This means practicing not only the physical action of your skill, but also practicing the internal environment that immediately precedes your skill execution.

I want you to basically work backward from whatever you're going to do in competition, to the degree that it is wise to do so in each training session. Obviously, an Ironman competitor is not going to run an Ironman every training day, but there are elements of preparation to practice. For example, are you practicing the transition in the same way you would execute it in a competition? How many reps are you experiencing that are immediately transferable into the competitive arena? The quality and intensity of your preparation can significantly influence how your preparation transfers to competition.

52

SUCCESS IS AN EVENT; EXCELLENCE IS A **PROCESS**

JAMES CLEAR, AUTHOR OF THE BESTSELLER *ATOMIC HABITS*, speaks to a notion that I have utilized throughout my consulting career: "Success is an event; excellence is a process." Many of the most successful coaches, athletes, and business leaders I've worked with embrace this as a foundational philosophy.

Many people, when looking into the future at something they would like to achieve, select some event in which they'd like to be successful.

"I'd like to be on the podium at the Olympics."
"I want to make the varsity team in tryouts."
"I want to win the club championship."

Having these aspirations can be motivating and inspiring, but the long-term growth potential that's inherent in the pursuit of excellence might get negated if we are only fixated on one point or one moment in time.

The onus is on you to put systems in place and build habits that are intentionally designed to foster your continual growth and development. This is how the best individuals in their respective businesses achieve highly in specific events and *also* sustain success over the long haul. They see the envisioned event as something that is just another valuable step along the never-ending road to greater knowledge and progress.

The greatest and most consistent dividends for any of us will be paid in the future based on how aware we can become of the mechanisms that guide us toward mastery and how disciplined we can be at executing on those mechanisms. This is the pathway upon which excellence is found, and this provides the greatest chance for success at individual events.

53

PRESSURE DOESN'T EXIST

IN THE WORLD OF SPORTS, "PRESSURE" IS A COMMONLY USED word. But when I ask people what they mean by "pressure," it's often very hard for them to define it. I will ask athletes, "Well, can you taste it? Do you smell it?"

"No," they will reply. "It's just a feeling that I get inside."

The feeling they are describing is the body's reaction. For most people, pressure is the sensation of particular feelings or sensations brought on by a certain situation. The situation generates a thought or an interpretation. And our thoughts generate either an emotional response or a physiological response. This is why I always use air quotes when I talk about "pressure."

I see pressure as a person's collective interpretation of a situation. It often comes about when athletes inadvertently increase their perceived demand on themselves beyond what is actually being asked of them. This can feed into an athlete being worried about whether or not the demand they perceive is going to outpace the resources they have.

Am I being asked to do something I'm not capable of doing?
Am I going to fail at this thing?
Will I be successful at all that is being asked of me right now?

If a basketball player is at the free throw line with the chance to win the world championship, shooting a free throw is not what's generating pressure for that individual. Shooting free throws is what they do every day of their life. **"Pressure" is the athlete's thoughts about what this free throw means. This thinking generates an internal environment and a collective energy around what this moment means, rather than what is required in this specific moment.**

To some extent, we can all appreciate what that moment feels like. I'm not suggesting that you don't ever feel pressure or that it's not a thing. But what I want you to understand is that pressure is not doing something to you. It's you doing it to yourself based on how you choose to think about the situation.

As you adjust and adapt to your thought processes, you become more mentally disciplined. You reframe and reinterpret situations, and what you feel inside becomes less and less debilitating to performance. It often doesn't go away completely, but the task becomes more prioritized or prominent.

You want to get into those highly relevant situations—that's why you work hard and train hard. When you find yourself there, it is helpful to have been working on being really clear about how you will choose to think or what senses you will choose to engage in a particular way in that situation. What are the thoughts that are helpful in coping with and taking advantage of these moments? What are the body sensations that are helpful (e.g., "feeling my tempo," "exhaling slowly," "exaggerating my knee bend")?

Remember, it's not the free throws doing it to you. The 10-foot putt is not doing it to you. Running the board meeting is not making you nervous. It is your choice to think certain nonproductive thoughts that generates what feels like pressure to you. Be very clear about what is *actually* being asked of you, and recognize how often you have all that it takes to be reasonably successful.

54

TASK ORIENTATION VS. EGO ORIENTATION

ONE OF THE BASIC ELEMENTS OF MENTAL TRAINING IS MAKING a distinction between task orientation and ego orientation. *Ego orientation* asks questions like:

> *How am I doing versus the people around me?*
> *How am I doing versus fellow competitors or even versus my own teammates?*

Ego orientation is almost entirely manifested and steeped in a me vs. them comparison.

Task orientation, on the other hand, is when someone is measuring themselves or their success against mastery at their skill. This involves asking questions like:

> *How am I getting better at this skill?*
> *Am I getting better at these tactics?*
> *Am I getting stronger at this exercise in the gym?*

In this case, it becomes more a case of me against myself yesterday, as I move toward excellence. This is very different from the ego orientation of "me vs. that person over there" and comparing yourself to how the other person is doing today or even last week.

In my experience in college athletics, and even in professional athletics, I have found that athletes inadvertently use ego orientation to support their confidence or belief. In the early days, this works out nicely for them because they're largely better than everybody around them. When I'm kicking everybody's butt in my community, or in my region, or even in my state, I'm bound to feel pretty good about myself.

However, when an athlete gets to the next level of play, if they're using that same metric for measuring their competency, it can become very confusing. All of a sudden, there are twenty players who were the best in their state, and now they're all on the same team. In this situation, it feels more like me vs. them. And as they're looking around, they don't feel very good about their own abilities, because these other athletes are actually better than they are, or the gap between themselves and others is not as great as they're used to seeing.

As a result of this, I am constantly talking to athletes about comparing themselves against themselves, comparing themselves against the demand of the sport or the demand of a particular skill acquisition. **Task orientation asks the athlete to measure progress differently, asking, "Did I beat what I did yesterday?" as opposed to "Am I better than her?"**

To be clear, there are some people who are extraordinarily successful using ego orientation. And there are some people who can be not only inspired, but ultimately grounded in ego orientation and experience high levels of success. To that effect, I'm not suggesting you avoid ego orientation altogether. And I'm not saying that having an ego orientation is not going to work out well for you. For some athletes, it drives them: *It's about me proving myself; it's about me being better than them; it's always about me competing with the people around me.* But I would argue it's a sliver of the population for which this is a prudent strategy. Moreover, if you can, at a minimum, join your ego orientation with task orientation, you are likely to feel a little less pressure. It can also help you contain the up-and-down bounce in confidence based on what the people around you are doing, over which you obviously have no control.

55

THOUGHT STOPPING

THE PRACTICE OF THOUGHT STOPPING INVOLVES A THREE-STEP process, so simple that it can be taught to little kids. It is a technique that was purportedly developed in the late 1950s by a psychiatrist named Dr. Joseph Wolpe. And it is a technique that some find very helpful.

1. Be aware of a thought that you're having.
2. If you don't like that thought, then literally say the word "stop" to yourself. (Some people will visualize a stop sign, a red light, or something that triggers an interruption of thought.)
3. Change your thought to something that's more productive.

With an unwanted thought, it's a process of awareness, followed by a literal "stop" phrase or picture, and then a shift to something more productive or constructive.

When I talk to athletes about this, I use the same elementary language. **Thought stopping is a simple but effective way to become more aware of unproductive internal dialogue.** The connection between thoughts, feelings, and behaviors is foundationally important.

If an athlete is struggling with this, I will often ask, "What if what you are thinking were to scroll across the scoreboard? What if everybody could see what you're thinking? Would you be okay with that? Is what you're saying to yourself productive, healthy, and favorable?"

For most athletes, the answer is, "I would *never* want someone to see what I'm actually thinking!"

So why would it be okay to allow those thoughts to go unchecked? Investigate why you are saying these things to yourself. Stop the internal feed that says, *You suck. Why are you so terrible? Oh my God, you're embarrassing yourself.*

Those thoughts that you would not want people to be aware of are probably not productive or helpful. Notice I am not saying that these thoughts are negative or bad. I'm not even saying that they're wrong.

Consider what you would want the scroll on the scoreboard to say instead: *You're fine. You've got this. You're better than this.*

This is not about judging thoughts as positive or negative; it's more of a pressure test: *Is this productive? Is this helpful? Not: Is this bad or wrong or negative?* Because sometimes people might see a thought as negative, but that type of thought might still be productive for that particular athlete. In the end, stop the thoughts that are not useful and replace them with words that help you function more effectively.

56

THE PROBLEM WITH POSITIVE AND NEGATIVE

WHAT ONE PERSON CONSIDERS POSITIVE, SOMEONE ELSE might see in a different way. Another person's negative might be neutral—or even helpful—for someone else. I've got nothing against positive thinking, but it can become toxic.

A lot of athletes adopt language like:

"I will be a champion."
"I will be first."
"I will get a college scholarship."
"I will win a medal."

Professionals sell the power of positive affirmations, encouraging people to "see it happen" and that sort of thing.

When somebody says "I will . . . " and there's a positive result attached to it, there's another part of the brain that can trigger a different question: "So what if you don't?" This can create an issue for some athletes.

Oftentimes these thoughts also create a positive expectation. A lot of people are sold on this positive version or vision of how things are going to turn out, you know, through God's will or through hard work or whatever. Everybody's got their spin on why it's going to be okay.

I don't sell the idea that it's going to be okay, because we don't know that it's going to be okay. What we are doing is working toward giving you the best chance for it to be okay and increasing the odds of it being okay. **Telling yourself that it's going to turn out in your favor can set you up for not just disappointment, but sometimes devastation.**

Parents can inadvertently fall into this trap. They adopt "positive" parenting, always telling their child that they're special, that it's all going to turn out in their favor. Then the child experiences the real world when it punches them in the face. A lot of kids haven't even developed coping mechanisms because they were so convinced it was going to all turn out well.

I'm not *anti*-positive. For some people, it works. For those who benefit from this approach, I would gladly sanction it. But for most, I think it is a double-edged sword.

If I had to use the term *negative*, whether it be negative language or negative self-talk, generally it's a put-down or something that's unproductive or unhelpful—it doesn't inspire the athlete in a healthy way. That sort of language I just don't see as productive. Work toward neutral, factual, objective language.

57

DISPUTE **THE STORIES** YOU TELL YOURSELF

DON'T BELIEVE EVERYTHING YOU THINK. AS HUMANS, WE HAVE a tendency to interpret what we encounter in our own unique way because we have our own unique filters. But that doesn't necessarily mean that what we are telling ourselves is objectively true. In fact, oftentimes it's not. Most of us are constantly making up stories in our head and acting upon them as if they are real. There are times when there is value and benefit to disputing the stories we are telling ourselves. Ask yourself, *Is what I'm thinking completely accurate? Are there alternative ways of thinking of this? Is there a different explanation that might make sense?*

This effort can be helpful to minimize the rabbit-hole thinking where one thing leads to another, which leads to another. If all of this happens without checking the accuracy of the initial premise, belief, or starting point, we put ourselves on a path that is not likely to be beneficial. We are often not in control of the first thoughts that pop into our minds, but we can take greater control through disciplined second and third thoughts that "fact-check" the truth and benefits of our first thought. **In taking the time to explore alternative explanations or perspectives, you can minimize the bias you bring to a situation.**

> The athlete thinks: *The coach didn't put me in the game. It's obvious the coach doesn't like me.*
>
> Let's turn the tables and consider it from the coach's perspective: *That athlete is not going hard today. It's obvious that she doesn't care—she is checked out.*

Is it true that the coach doesn't like the athlete? Is it true that the athlete doesn't care? In either case, there are other ways to look at it. Be willing to question the original story or interpretation and fact-check for alternatives.

These types of "stories," formulated by the beholder's opinion, can then be acted upon in ways that almost begin to create truth to their stories. The athlete who the coach "doesn't like" begins to act aloof or detached, which decreases the coach's appreciation of that athlete's interactions. And so on . . .

On a daily basis, I am helping my clients closely examine the messages or stories they are telling themselves, and I'm exposing them to alternate explanations. I do this to help guide them toward a more objective and neutral view of situations and/or to direct them to ask themselves questions that clarify possible misconceptions.

Even with a second party to help facilitate your consideration of replacement interpretations, this is challenging work. It can be difficult to do alone. While I appreciate that this isn't an easy task, the benefits of closely examining your interpretations and attendant actions can be vast. I believe you will also find that with practice, disputing the stories you tell yourself will positively influence your internal dialogue and emotional state.

58

ACCEPT YOUR **HUMANITY**

IN DEALING WITH HIGH-PROFILE ATHLETES AND, FRANKLY, athletes of any level, I am often confronted with a high level of perfectionism or self-deprecation. In either case, my clients are effectively frustrated with themselves over a lack of skill, consistency, or success. It might be the case that they have what others see as a level of success or growth and yet they don't own it as such. This is because they're so focused on what they're not yet doing that they don't appreciate what they *are* currently doing in terms of their sport performance.

Sometimes I get feedback from an athlete like, "It was just so hard because I did all this work, and then it didn't turn out very well."

I will respond, "Of course this is disappointing, but also it sounds like it's difficult for you to accept your humanity. It's a challenge for you to recognize that as humans, we make mistakes, even when we've trained well and even when we're highly accomplished."

Early in my career, I traveled with professional tennis players from tournament to tournament. I had one young player in particular who was constantly frustrated. No matter what he accomplished, he continued to hold himself to an unsustainable standard. He was asked to go to Tampa to play a couple practice sets with Pete Sampras, who at the time was ranked No. 1 in the world. I videoed the session, and the athlete I was working with hit a couple shots that Pete Sampras swung at and completely missed. To be clear, it wasn't like Pete shanked the ball off the frame or hit it poorly. He simply swung and missed. And it wasn't because the ball he was trying to hit was screaming fast or doing something crazy—it's relatively rare for somebody at that level to find themselves in that situation, let alone when that athlete is No. 1 in the world and in the prime of his career.

In the years that followed, I showed clips of that video to many young tennis players. The lesson was, "Look, here's a guy who at the time had won more Grand Slams than any tennis player in human history. And here's a guy who can swing and miss. So, if he can do something as elementary as swing and miss, you can certainly make mistakes yourself."

The best athletes in the world, even at their best, will do things that are not perfect, whether it be in sport or out of sport. The better athletes make mistakes and acknowledge that it's part of being human—they humbly accept the reality that they are not perfect. Furthermore, they do not over-rotate when they make mistakes. Sampras didn't melt down or beat himself up when he missed the ball—he was absolutely nonplussed. In fact, he laughed out loud.

It was as if Sampras was surprised, and in my mind that makes sense. There's an anticipation that I'm going to, at a minimum, touch the ball, right? When it doesn't happen, the response is, *Whoa, that was weird*, as opposed to some sort of self-indictment: *What's wrong with me?*

Over the years, as I've talked about this, people have responded, "Well, of course Sampras can blow it off because he was one of the best in the world and he knew how good he was—having banked so many successes, he knew that was a one-off experience."

While I believe there's validity in that perspective, I don't think it cheapens or mitigates fully the demonstration that if the best in the world can learn to live with their mistakes, so can those of us who are not the best in the world. **That lack of grace for ourselves as imperfect humans comes at a cost. No matter how hard we try or how much we train, we are going to make mistakes and we are going to fail at times.**

Athletes often have a skewed perception: *To beat this person, I need to execute this way every time and I cannot make mistakes.* And this is completely irrational. Nobody out there, even at the pro level, can do that. When such a perception becomes the standard, it's an impossible ask, even for a professional athlete. Work toward acceptance and humility.

59

HUMAN BEING VS. HUMAN DOING

ONE OF THE GREATEST CHALLENGES IS FOR ATHLETES TO SEPARATE their identity as a person from the actions and behaviors and accomplishments they elicit in their sport environment. The same is true with any profession—attorney, physician, mental coach, etc. Most of us tend to weave our accomplishments, or what we do, into our identity. This is particularly challenging at the highest levels of sport because the outcomes and results are tangible and oftentimes very public. Particularly when you know people are watching, it's easy to weld your performance in sport with your identity, and before long, it's a case of "As goes my sport performance, so I go... If I have a good day, I feel good about myself. If I have a bad day, I feel poorly about myself—I don't just feel poorly about my performance, but about *myself*."

I've watched as many athletes in the midst of their sport experience attempt to figure out how to separate what they do from who they are as a person. If they don't figure it out somewhere along the way, once that athlete's career in sports is over, there's a monumental challenge around identity. "I was Jeff the baseball player, and now I'm just Jeff, and I don't even know who I am anymore!" The same goes for anyone who retires from any profession because up until that point, what they do has been intertwined with who they are.

Even with young athletes, 8–10 years old, I talk about making the distinction between you as a person and your performance. I'm especially focused on communicating this to parents. Inadvertent comments are regularly made around games and competition, such as, "You are amazing!" Rather than saying, "Hey, that was a really good performance today," performance becomes implicit in identity. Ultimately, this creates a threat to identity. Now my identity is on the line in my sport experience, rather than my sport experience being independent of me. This often translates into competitive anxiety and worry.

I ask athletes to think and speak about it this way: "I'm a person who ran a mile in under four minutes." This means that whatever my accomplishments may be, who I am as a person is independent and separate. Literally saying these words out loud, adopting this sort of language and thinking, helps to make the internal distinction between being and doing.

You are a human being, and that's independent of your actions, independent of what you do. People find it difficult to resist self-identifying with their accomplishments. "I'm a great parent," "I'm a great cook" . . . this might seem simplistic, but I'd rather you think of yourself as a person who parents well, or a person who cooks well. It's normal to label ourselves based on what we do, but be intentional about making this distinction, constantly checking in with yourself.

I want you to be good with who you are as a person, independent of what you accomplished today. Otherwise, you are buckled in on a roller-coaster ride where your self-worth is tied to your most recent performance. Now it's not only the game that didn't go well; you're also feeling badly about yourself as a person.

One Day Better drives this point home by emphasizing the consistent effort to act in a way that aligns with your values and who you see yourself to be. What you do reflects who you are, but it is not ultimately who you are. Commit to making that critical distinction.

60

IN YOUR BODY, IN YOUR TARGET, OR **IN YOUR MIND?**

WITH ATHLETES, ONE OF THE VERY FIRST THINGS WE TALK ABOUT is *conscious competency*—being aware of those things that help you be your best. An example of this is an awareness of where you want to direct your attention immediately preceding execution.

For some people, having their attention in their body—a kinesthetic awareness—works best:

I'm feeling really grounded on the floor.
I want to feel my hip load in my backswing.
I want to really feel power through my pedals.

Kinesthetic body awareness helps drive performance for that athlete.

For another athlete, it's not tied to being in their body or what their body is feeling, but simply attaching to the target with clarity. Just envisioning the finish line is what gets some athletes to the finish line. For some golfers, being "in the hole" is the trick—they're not thinking about feeling anything in their body or how to roll the putt; they're just locked in on where the ball goes, into the hole.

For other people, it's more about having some sort of cue or phrase in their mind that captures what they would like to have happen.

In golf, we talk about swing thoughts, or some thought that triggers an action that is exactly what works for the golfer. But for others, the suggestion of a swing thought is a nonstarter because they are trying not to think about anything, and that may be exactly what works for you!

There's value in understanding what body orientation, target orientation, mantra, cue, or thought triggers consistent performance. It's generally not all of the above. It's most likely one of those that falls within a particular domain. There might be a couple of things in the body (vision and feel) or a few target types that work well, and you might find yourself mixing those together. But it's more often the case that people are using too many of those sorts of cues simultaneously and/or randomly. This can fray attention and ultimately compromise the stability of your internal environment and its ability to manifest consistent performance.

Self-awareness is essential here, as I believe that the athlete often knows best. It can be hard at times for some coaches or parents to be flexible enough to consider all possible paths to performance and teach, value, and nurture this in an athlete. Work with the athlete to help them discover what is most effective.

61

THE POWER OF NEUTRAL THINKING

ONE THING THAT COMES AS A SURPRISE TO MOST OF MY CLIENTS early in our conversations is the fact that I'm not a strong advocate of positive thinking. Many people think that's what mental trainers do—help people think positively. To be clear: I'm certainly not *against* positive thinking, and I'm absolutely against negative thinking. If thinking positively is helpful to an athlete, I will guide them to that sort of self-talk. However, I've found it more useful to guide most athletes to neutral thinking.

To my knowledge, the concept of neutral thinking was formally introduced in public forums by my protégé Trevor Moawad in his book *It Takes What It Takes*. Trevor did an amazing job of articulating the value and benefits of neutral thinking, and I want to keep large concepts reasonably short here, but I highly recommend Trevor's book.

Whenever an athlete has a negative thought about something, I want them to "pressure-test" that thought in this way: *Is this thought factually accurate (true) and objective, or is it an opinion?* I want them to work to make sure that what they are saying to themselves are things that are objectively true, even if what is being said is not preferred. Describing things as they are without attendant judgment or evaluation can be difficult. Let's consider a couple of examples.

A golfer hits a tee shot left into the trees:

Negative thoughts: *My driver is terrible. My swing is off again today. I'm going to make bogie at best from there.*

Neutral thoughts: *My ball went almost straight left. Obviously, I'm better at swinging my driver than that. There was something wrong with that particular swing or it wouldn't have gone over there, but I don't want to make it bigger than it is. Let's go see where my ball is and prepare well to give myself a chance to hit a quality second shot.*

The mistake is isolated, which prevents the athlete from questioning their swing in general.

A triathlete has a training session wherein they didn't hit their desired training numbers:

Negative thoughts: *I'm never going to be competitive if I train like this. My competitors are crushing their workouts and I'm struggling to complete this one. What if I can't execute this week as planned?*

Neutral thoughts: *I didn't hit the numbers in my workout I wanted to. Of course this is disappointing, but everyone has challenging days. Let's get quality rest and see what we learn tomorrow. If this continues, I will talk with my coach to figure out what adjustments to make. As for my competitors, I don't know how anyone else's workouts are going.*

Ultimately, we have the option to speak to ourselves and interpret things any way we want to. A big part of any athlete's job is to hold themselves accountable to productive and helpful neutral language. If they happen to tell themselves positive things, that's just fine too!

62

DO SOMETHING... ANYTHING!

WHEN PEOPLE FEEL ANXIOUS, FEARFUL, OR WORRIED, THERE can be a tendency to default to inertia. People are wired differently, so other people might be reasonably impulsive or spontaneous in such a situation. However scattered or random their response, it can sometimes work for them. But far more people err on the side of being cautious, even to the point where they don't move—they are almost literally paralyzed, like a deer in the headlights.

Sometimes the inertia is metaphorical, and the athlete is caught in the indecision of which pathway to take: *I'm having a problem right now, and whether it's related to sport performance, strategy, tactics, or a mechanical adjustment, something doesn't feel like it's working.*

It might be a relational issue that freezes an athlete or coach: *I'm not sure how to reconcile or how to manage this well.*

People often remain stuck in what they're doing, caught in a pattern of spinning, thinking about their problem and wondering which of the potential pathways leads to a solution. When these individuals come to me, they have a clear agenda. First, they will ask me, "Can you open up a path for me that I might not be seeing?" And if that leaves them empty-handed, they ask, "Can you guide me down the right path?" By now you are likely well aware that I believe there is no one "right" path.

My advice is to suggest that the client be thoughtful and deliberate about moving in some direction, one that allows them to gather more information. You can always pivot from a path that doesn't feel like it's working. Or you can gather information that it *is* working and continue down that path. **If you have a tendency to worry about whether you are on the right path, that worry is likely to keep you stuck**, and now once again you are either literally or metaphorically not moving forward, lingering in the same problem.

What is stopping you from taking the first step? Some athletes or coaches are not willing to try a particular solution. They might tell me:

"I don't think that's going to work out very well."
"I know somebody who tried that, and it didn't work for them."
"I'm scared that if I do this, certain people will think less of me."

There can be countless excuses or reasons people cling to in justifying why they won't move when they're stuck.

If you're lost in the woods, once you've done all you can to navigate and you still really don't know where you are, you might be tempted to sit there for a while and hope to be rescued. But when it becomes apparent there's no rescue effort underway, it's time for action. Set a trail and mark it so you can backtrack and go somewhere else if necessary. You know where you're going, you know where you've been, and you can always go back and start new with something else.

Once people get some momentum, they navigate a path for themselves through the labyrinth, or the house of mirrors that a problem presents, maybe even with some help from a friend or a coach or a guide. **More often, the solution is found in being brave enough to break inertia with some sort of action. You can always come back and try another method.**

In talking with athletes, I've been known to challenge their excuses with, "You don't require more information; the situation requires more courage."

Some people inadvertently choose the pain that they're stuck in instead of the uncertainty of the path. "I'm familiar with this pain . . . it's cold, and it's dark, and it's scary, but I know what it is. I *don't* know what's out there. So I'll just sit here."

Do something—anything—and you will have learned something. You might screw up, but you will have data on what doesn't work, and from there you can begin again.

63

BUILD A CASE BEFORE MAKING A CORRECTION

THERE ARE A LOT OF PEOPLE WHO ARE LOATH TO MAKE A correction. They will stick with their process and ride that metaphorical horse, even if the horse's legs are broken. At the other extreme, we can find people who are constantly course correcting and doing so without having the data to support whether or not a course correction is justified. The world of golf illustrates this well because golfers, even those who are amazingly accomplished and incredibly proficient at what they do, are prone to tinker endlessly with their mechanics and their technique: *The ball is going a little bit left today, so maybe I need to do this instead.* They start making adjustments, and pretty soon they're trying to correct something in their swing when there was nothing wrong with it in the first place. Thus, they've effectively created a second problem.

I watch a volleyball player take a swing, and the ball is hit out of bounds. Now all of a sudden, you can see the athlete moving their arm in some sort of a correction as if, "Oh, that was wrong." On one hand, we want them to feel the correct motion. However, I don't want the athlete thinking about changing their natural way of attacking the ball, because that hit might have been a one-off. Maybe they hit two in a row that don't go very well. In these situations, I tell people,

"You would make a terrible attorney—you still have too little evidence, and you're trying to make a whole case out of it!" I want to gather more evidence before considering or attempting a correction.

Once you can make a case for suggesting a correction, then make the adjustment. If you're constantly course correcting, you will never get to know what really works for you because your process is continually in flux. Rather than fixating on a correction, we want to stay the course until you have enough information that something is not working. At that point, you can make an intelligent correction based on gathered evidence, not one based on emotion or fear or anxiety. An athlete will think, *Oh no, something is wrong!* It could be the case that that particular swing was not good, but it doesn't mean something's wrong with your swing.

If you're conducting a scientific experiment, you have to keep everything the same to know what works. Suddenly or impulsively change dependent variables, and now all of your data is less helpful.

The best athletes are adapting constantly, but they're taking in new information and making intelligent adaptations. This is very different from a course correction or a mechanical correction based on tiny bits of data and triggered by anxiety or worry! The sport experience is fluid, requiring rational adaptation. Don't panic and make a change because something is not going the way you want it to go. Stop and ask:

What's driving the correction or adaptation?
Have I gathered intelligent data?
Am I making a wise and intelligent decision?
Is my action or correction driven by emotion, like fear or anxiety or worry?

Sometimes it's restlessness or impatience that is driving the change, or perhaps a lack of commitment to the process. There will be times when fear or worry may feel warranted, but grabbing at solutions that aren't *real* or deeply considered might only take you farther off the path.

You want to have a lot of information that what you're doing isn't working. Faced with that situation, fear might lead to inertia . . . or it might lead to impetuousness. Which of these two responses are you most likely to react with? What sorts of situations drive these responses? Engage in self-reflection and resist the urge to just make something up—**be thoughtful, be rational, be intelligent about how you proceed with adaptations and adjustments.**

64

I CARE, BUT IT DOESN'T MATTER

I HAVE JOKED WITH MANY ATHLETES OVER THE YEARS THAT this would be a phrase to tattoo on your body—and much to my chagrin, it happened when one of my clients did so!

I regularly hear athletes say that they run into emotional problems when they try too hard or put significant meaning into a contest or a training session. Inevitably, some athletes will suggest that they play better when they don't care, commenting, "Maybe I need to just *not care* and then I will relax and play better."

Because most athletes are deeply invested in their sport experience, it is improbable that they truly "do not care." Being excellent at any craft necessitates a great deal of caring. Athletes have to care to prepare well, stay engaged and focused, and regulate their internal environment to give themselves the best chance to be successful.

Instead of feigning indifference, I suggest that athletes recognize that they can reduce how much something matters to them by bringing a healthier perspective to it. Athletes at every level achieve superior performances by caring deeply, but also recognizing that while the contest might be important, in the long-term scheme of life, it likely doesn't matter much.

When we dig into what really matters, nearly everyone can make a distinction between the things that really matter and those that maybe don't matter quite as much. The things that truly matter to most athletes—their health, their family, their relationships, and so on—can be separated in their minds from the weight of a given contest or goal. I don't care if it's the Super Bowl, the US Open, the Kona Ironman . . . in the grand scheme of your life, I would argue that it doesn't matter. However, of course you care.

I want every athlete to work hard to keep their athletic experience in proper context. For many of the athletes I work with, sport is their life's work and certain contests hold significant influence over many things in their life. However, **remembering, "I care, but it doesn't matter," can help the athlete sustain both their inspiration and their motivation, without the added pressure of it mattering too much.**

Maybe you missed a PR this week or came up short of the podium—yes, it's painful and it sucks. And the outcome or result might temporarily matter financially and emotionally, but as it relates to life in general, I want to make sure you're holding on to caring but also recognizing that it doesn't matter. This mindset also opens up an athlete to acceptance of the possibility of losing in a more gracious and healthy manner, or keeping perspective about an outcome or situation that might initially feel like catastrophic failure.

65

ANTICIPATE VS. EXPECT

IN MY WORK WITH ATHLETES, I EMPHASIZE THAT *ANTICIPATION* is more about a belief that something is likely to happen and/or could conceivably happen, whereas *expectation* is a belief that something *will* happen. This is why I want athletes to anticipate success—to see it as a possibility, as something likely or plausible. I do not prefer that the athletes I work with have expectations—particularly in relation to any sort of outcome over which they do not have complete control.

Why is this distinction important? I have seen countless athletes, teams, or coaches go into a situation with an expectation that things are going to go their way, only to see them experience something unexpected and crumble, panic, or lose emotional control. Not getting what you expect can be disorienting, confusing, and discouraging because an expectation is something you convince yourself will happen—and when it doesn't, it can be a real motivation killer.

On the other hand, not getting what you anticipate means you've left open the door to the possibility that the success you were hoping for may not happen. While still staying optimistic and having belief, athletes are more inclined to trigger coping mechanisms, solutions, adjustments, or adaptations when adversity hits or things don't go as anticipated, because they did not initially convince themselves that the best outcomes would absolutely happen.

Having a deep expectation that something desired will happen often generates "oh shit" moments for athletes during their performance. **Anticipating without expecting allows for belief but also makes room for a resilient and flexible mindset when things go sideways,** leading toward a higher likelihood of emotional stability and intelligent adaptations.

66

THE ONLY ACCEPTABLE **EXPECTATIONS**

LET'S EXPLORE A FURTHER DISTINCTION BETWEEN ANTICIPATION and expectation. My typical rule with athletes and coaches is to have no concrete outcome expectations. As put forward in "Anticipate vs. Expect," I see this as a setup for a dysregulated internal environment when things don't go well. Predicting or expecting any particular outcome can also limit upside possibilities. There are innumerable times when athletes diminish their upside potential because they are expecting things to be different and they fail to recognize pathways for even greater successes.

Consequently, I promote a mindset around expectation: Expect things to be difficult, expect things to be different than you thought they would be, and expect the unexpected.

Many of the individuals who coach and consult with athletes sell the concept that having expectations that things are going to go your way will *inevitably* lead to success and that you will experience a favorable flow with adequate preparation or mentally sound practices. It's been my experience, however, that athletes are more likely to respond intelligently and optimally if they know in advance that something is likely to be very difficult and/or nonpreferred. In these situations, when encountering difficulty, the athlete is more likely to respond with something like, "Okay, here's one of the difficult things that I knew might happen. How can I respond to this in the best way possible?" They are already aware that coping with adversity is part of the experience, so they don't freak out when things "hit the fan." Instead, they start implementing coping strategies.

When you expect the contest or training session to go a certain way, it sets up the brain to be distracted or triggered. It's better to go into situations being at peace with the full spectrum of possibilities rather than having predicted any particular circumstance. This way, it's more likely that your internal switch will flip to acceptance rather than unpleasant surprise. We generally are looking to enhance the likelihood that you can respond to "what is" as opposed to being distracted by how you "wish it was." After all, wishing is a terrible mental strategy.

Instead of wishing things were different or being unpleasantly surprised when things go poorly, arm yourself with coping strategies for those inevitable moments in sport (and life!) when things don't go according to plan or preference, and start your training session or contest with acceptance of any possible outcome and an expectation that you will face difficulties.

67

PACE YOURSELF

WE TEND TO BRING UNREALISTIC EXPECTATIONS TO HOW LONG something will take. Mastery is an ambitious goal, but we can lack patience for the process. The quickened pace at which people expect things to happen is markedly different today in part as a result of technology. Information and experiences are instantly available in daily life.

Recently, I was describing to some college athletes how I used to listen to the radio hoping to hear my favorite song. If I happened to step away and miss it, it felt devastating because I probably wasn't going to hear it that day. In an "on-demand" world, if we want to listen to a song, we can hear it instantly and repeat it as often as we want.

There is no instant gratification in sports. To progress, you have to pace yourself in a way that is realistic relative to how quickly you can develop and how quickly you can acquire the skill. I encounter a lot of athletes who have an irrational notion about the speed at which skill acquisition occurs. Part of the challenge here is that oftentimes skill acquisition starts off at a rapid pace. From there, the gains may come in smaller increments. Skill acquisition typically plateaus, and grinding out the last subtle nuances of a skill generally takes a lot longer than the initial 30 percent.

The lack of willingness to pace oneself oftentimes leads people to try harder or do more in ways that are nonproductive. They can end up getting frustrated and annoyed because they're not growing at the rate that they once were. **Understand that growth requires a certain rhythm, a certain pace and understanding. It's going to take a while to interpret the growth curve in a way that's as accurate and objective as possible.**

For those athletes who are further along in the skill acquisition spectrum, impatience with the pace of development can result in an increasing number of overuse injuries, stress fractures, and stress reactions—the sorts of things that only further delay growth. The athlete is thinking, *It's not coming fast enough—that must mean I need to do more.*

Sometimes doing more is the answer. And sometimes doing more is exactly how you injure yourself or delay your developmental process.

Alternatively, sometimes the impatience with the speed of the process triggers reduced motivation or discouragement. In these situations, the athlete's exasperation with the pace of progress can influence their focus, determination, and ultimately be the reason they leave the sport completely.

Maintaining a realistic perspective of the pace of development can keep you working in the sport and doing so in a way that minimizes the risk that you will abandon the journey or inadvertently harm yourself.

68

THE ROLE OF VISION IN **ATTENTIONAL CONTROL**

YOU CAN REGAIN ATTENTIONAL CONTROL BY BEING VERY detailed about exactly what you are seeing. If I'm on the tennis court, I might direct my attention to something narrow and right in front of me—not just the tennis ball in my hand, but the fuzz on the tennis ball and the texture of its seams. My attention is fixed on intricate details.

Brain science has shown that in moments like this, brain-wave activity slows down, which benefits attention. Overthinking takes place in the prefrontal cortex. When we stop overthinking, our capacity to focus improves. **Looking at something and being intentional about picking out the details and sustaining that attention for an extended period of time can bring you back to the present moment.** What you are looking at begins to "pop," and you can better distinguish the foreground from the background, truly seeing things in 3D, picking out the color nuances, observing the details. By returning to the present, you can get your focus back to the task at hand.

So much of the brain is directed and influenced by vision, and the brain functions like a prediction machine. We're always on the lookout for threats; we're hardwired to survive. When we start getting unfocused and our attention begins to drift, it's possible to bring our attention back to something that's essentially safe and right in front of us. Looking at the tennis ball is safe, so we can calm down and be more centered.

Another application of attentional control involves relevant cues. Making sure I'm picking up on the spin of the ball as it's coming toward me uses my vision to elicit improved sport performance. The more we hone our vision and our ability to pick up those nuances, the more likely we will be productive. **Having clarity about where to direct your vision can position you to receive the earliest and best clues that will help your decision-making and direct your action.**

Early in my career, we developed a way to train visual acuity and eye control in tennis players. We filled a basket with three different colors of tennis balls, and the coach would rapid-feed the player balls in random order, which didn't give the athlete much time to pick out the color from the baseline. The instruction was for the player to hit the two-toned ball down the line, hit the white ball cross-court, and with the yellow ball hit a drop shot. This forced the athlete's attention to truly see the ball, because they wouldn't know what to do with the ball unless they could discern the color as quickly as possible. We came to realize the impact of this training when a player got into a match, having trained themselves to be truly locked in on seeing the ball. The athletes were picking up spin better, which is an obvious advantage, creating time for an adaptation or micro adjustment.

For baseball players, being able to pick up on the spin of the ball as it's coming at them can lead to massive improvements in their ability to discern a fastball from a breaking ball—even if they see it just a millisecond faster.

Let's consider a sport like swimming. There's always something you can sight, whether it's staring at the feet of the athlete in front of you or homing in on the lane line every third breath. In situations like this, you are using your vision just for a moment, focused on catching that glimpse in a rhythmic fashion. Your eyes are fixed on that space, and more of your thoughts are directed toward picking up on the vivid detail. This is what it looks like to practice attentional control—you can fill your mind with what you're seeing.

Once again, the inverse can be true as well. In a moment that feels overwhelming or difficult, it might be the case that you want to close your eyes and no longer use your vision. There will be times when what we see is not helping us become more attentive—it's distracting us and leading us to become more anxious. If you are walking into an arena filled with 100,000 people, you could find yourself becoming overwhelmed. Close your eyes and now you are in your breath, and all of a sudden what's happening around you is more muted and your attention is focused internally. There are different tools for each situation. Recognize the power of vision to shift attention and use it to your advantage.

69

THE FIRST DOMINO

MANY OF US PLAYED WITH DOMINOS AS CHILDREN. AS WE GROW older, there are multiple games that can be played with dominos, with many different variations. When we are younger, the predominant game is to position the dominos in a winding line on some sort of surface. Once we have used up all our dominos, we gently push the first domino, setting off a chain reaction that knocks down each domino in succession. How delightful!

I use this metaphor often in my work with athletes. One of the bigger challenges for athletes in multiple domains is that there is a tendency to overthink the technical or mechanical elements of the tasks in their sport. Golfers and baseball and softball batters overthink their swings. Tennis and volleyball and pickleball players overthink their serves. Basketball, hockey, lacrosse, and field hockey athletes overthink their shots.

I guide athletes to evolve to the point where these tasks become automatic. As athletes become more proficient and get more experience, this objective becomes more and more likely to become realized. However, in individuals who are in the developmental stages, and even among those at the top of their respective sports, there are times where the mind is cluttered with too many sequential steps.

Get clear about what is your first domino. **Working to discover the initial body sensation or thought or action that triggers the domino effect, or the rest of your execution, is a critical tool to have in your toolbox.** For some athletes, the initial domino remains somewhat the same over their careers. However, most athletes find that the initial "thing" that triggers successful performance might vary from time to time. The swing thought or feel that might work one week for a PGA Tour golfer might not have the same effect a few weeks later. In my experience, if the athlete is diligent about seeking that "first domino," they will often find a sense of peace and security from having a go-to task to put their attention toward when they are under stress.

Locate your first domino—the one that is currently generating successful execution—and watch the cascade of successes that follow it.

70

THE STRONGEST DON'T ALWAYS SURVIVE

THE COMMONLY QUOTED DARWINIAN NOTION THAT "THE STRONGEST will survive" is only part of the story. While it is true that those athletes with the greatest physical and mental strength are often at or near the top of their sport, Charles Darwin purported that those species which thrived were the ones that were most effective at adaptation. I have found this to be the case in sport as well.

The athletes who go into their training sessions, preparation segments, and competitive situations with a clear intention to adapt and flex to what they encounter are the ones I see skyrocket in their respective endeavors. Rather than getting sidetracked by wishing things were different, or being upset or distracted by circumstances not being as they'd expected, **these athletes are the ones who size up the situation and adapt creatively and flexibly to be the best they can be in that moment within the given circumstances.**

I regularly speak to golfers about how to embrace rainy, challenging conditions, to tennis players about adjusting their play for the wind, or to triathletes on adapting to poor course management or extreme weather conditions. The athletes who actively seek opportunities to practice adaptation—whether in a singular moment in practice or in competition, or in a macro sense as their entire sport evolves—are the ones who manage to capture their share of successes.

On the other hand, I've seen some incredibly skilled and well-prepared athletes get beaten because of their lack of adaptation. On paper they are the stronger athletes in the field. It could be that they are held back by a sense of rigidity or stubbornness or an unwillingness to change for any number of reasons. For some it's because "I've always done it this way." For others it is because "I shouldn't have to change." For still others it is overconfidence—they don't have to change because they will just beat everyone anyway. There are a multitude of explanations or excuses for an athlete's unwillingness to adjust or perceived inability to adapt.

In the end, among athletes whose physical and mental skills are somewhat equal, the athletes with a mindset geared toward adaptation increase their likelihood of surviving longer.

You can choose to cultivate an adaptation mindset today by openly seeking opportunities to make adjustments.

71

PLAY YOUR HIGHLIGHT REEL

THERE IS VALUE AND BENEFIT TO USING IMAGERY AND VISUALIZATION, though in my own anecdotal evidence, this tool is only minimally effective when it is focused on visualizing successful outcomes in the future. I've found that many athletes have a hard time imagining their future experiences in a completely positive light, so for some, this type of visualization can generate future-tripping anxiety. If you can visualize yourself winning the golf tournament or hitting the baseball over the fence, keep doing it. Future-based, success-oriented imagery unlocks confidence and success for some athletes, but for plenty of others it has a neutral or potentially negative effect.

In my experience, imagery is more powerful when you are recalling events that have actually happened. Replaying successes that are already embedded and experienced can bring an athlete back to that moment—what they were thinking, what they did, and how it felt.

"Highlight-reel" imagery allows you to remember and relive the moments when things went well in a training session, practice, or competition. For most athletes, it is relatively easy to remember these occasions. Some athletes can conjure up vivid recollections, drawing on many of their senses. I encourage you to take the time to be intentional with your historical moments of success so that you can effectively flood your mind with those thoughts, feelings, and pictures as gathered evidence of what you are capable of achieving. Remembering what you have done often feels more concrete and significant than what you hope to do in a future situation.

Start by making time to create an intentional list of specific successes. These can be a solitary moment (e.g., hitting a good shot, executing something well in practice) or a larger macro moment (e.g., crossing the finish line after a long race). Use these questions to collect vivid details:

- What did it feel like in those moments?
- What were your emotions?
- What were you hearing?
- What do you remember seeing?

By being purposeful about anchoring and banking those moments, athletes report that it becomes easier to recollect these positive reminders during difficult moments. **Use your highlight reels to intentionally cue belief and confidence in challenging situations.**

72

TRUST ME... OR DON'T

MANY COACHES WILL CLAIM THAT IT'S A LACK OF TRUST THAT keeps athletes from achieving their goals. "Trust your training, trust your technique, trust the strategy." Taking that a step further, what many coaches are really saying is: *Trust me.* It's a tall order, and it begs the question of how essential it is for an athlete to trust their coach.

We have a tendency in sport to use the terms *trust* and *commitment* interchangeably. Trust and commitment are closely aligned, but they are distinct concepts that are not synonymous. Trust is a valuable commodity that often leads to breakthrough performances; however, many athletes approach their sport from a place of distrust or defensiveness or hesitation. How can coaches help these athletes?

My answer to this question might come as a huge relief. The best way forward in this high-stakes relationship is for a coach to say: "Whether you trust it or not, and whether you trust me or not, commit to the process." I've worked with a lot of coaches and athletes who make the mistake of demanding trust, and they often end up stuck in indecision and frustration. In reality, it is *commitment* that is nonnegotiable. After all, if an athlete isn't going to commit to the training program, how can you ever know whether it's working?

The athlete's hesitation reveals how trust works as a double-edged sword in the coach–athlete relationship. Many athletes find themselves waiting to commit fully to the coach's program until trust is established. Consequently, when adjustments are made to the training program, the athlete isn't fully sure that they will work. And it will come as no surprise that those adjustments are less likely to work because the athlete is not fully committed.

Coaches would do well to give their athletes the latitude to not trust. Instead, the coach can ask the athlete to simply commit to the process of implementing the changes that might lead to improved performance, both on a macro and micro level, independent of trusting it.

When trust is an expectation from the onset of a coach–athlete relationship, it can cause a great deal of frustration on both sides. The athlete might ask for evidence or data on why a given approach works, which may cause their coach to feel the lack of trust. If the coach responds to the doubt by being firm and authoritative, or maybe not even recognizing the athlete's lack of trust, it might cause the athlete to become more resistant.

As a coach, it helps to keep in mind that the same traits that cause athletes to occasionally second-guess their coach—some level of compulsion and obsession—are what sport is all about; it's how world champions are made. **When the expectation is shifted to commitment, the pursuit of performance becomes a collaborative effort involving both coach and athlete.** It's possible to gather more "clean data" about whether or not a given change is positively impacting the desired performance metrics when the athlete is fully committed to executing the prescribed process.

As a coach, when you ask the athlete to commit, you are asking them to act in a particular way for a particular period of time. Perhaps you have outlined a race strategy for a 10K. The athlete learns nothing if they abandon the effort after 5K because it doesn't seem to be working. But if the athlete can commit to the strategy for the full 10K, knowing that if it does not pay off there will be an open discussion with the coach about a potential future adjustment to be made, they are more likely to commit fully.

Let us also consider that commitment works both ways. How much does a coach trust their athlete? How committed is a coach to the athlete's experience if they don't really trust that the athlete is going to do the right thing, or is even willing to be coached? Worse yet, what if a coach gets to the point where they question whether the athlete is "worth their time"?

I've found myself in multiple situations where coaches have expressed these sorts of sentiments to me. They find themselves inclined to put their energy into other athletes who seem to have more potential or "want it more." Some of these coaches have relied on "strong-arm tactics" in working with their athletes, and when an athlete doesn't respond well, the coach's commitment to the athlete wavers.

One of the most pleasurable things I've experienced in my career is watching some of these coaches choose to hang in there with those athletes and commit to their development. In time, they learned that they could, in fact, trust that things would work out for these athletes. I can recall multiple instances where the athlete rose to the upper echelons of their sport, far beyond where the coach thought they could go. The athlete's success demanded a commitment from the coach, in advance of the coach trusting whether these athletes could get there.

Just as with athletes, the same holds true for coaches. To provide the athlete with the greatest opportunity to manifest their potential, it helps if the coach is all in on the training regimen and their attention to the athlete, independent of their opinion of how it's going to turn out.

73

GIVE 100%
OF WHATEVER YOU HAVE IN YOUR TANK

MANY ATHLETES AND COACHES (AND NEARLY ALL HUMANS) have a tendency to sometimes be distracted by things that are less than optimal:

> "I'm really not feeling well-rested today."
> "My legs are really tired."
> "I'm still a little sore in my shoulder."
> "I don't feel as fit or ready as I was hoping to be by today's contest."

When confronted by these sorts of "limitations," how do you choose to respond?

The best of the best learn to accept that with whatever percentage they have on a given day, they are going to give 100% effort. That is absolutely all that they can do, and worrying about what they *don't have* is counterproductive and distracting.

Only feeling 70% healthy or ready? Then give 100% of that 70%. Most athletes allow the 30% they are *not feeling* to influence the quality of the 70% they *are*. The athletes or coaches or businesspeople who are exceptionally disciplined mentally will not allow the 70% that they *are* to be influenced by the 30% they *are not*.

While everyone prefers to be 100% fit and sharp and rested every time, the reality is that it is an extremely rare day when this is true. For the vast majority of days, you can live well with a clear intention to give 100% of what it is that you have in the tank that day, rather than lamenting what is missing.

Find satisfaction in giving all you have rather than being distracted by wishing you had more.

74

"FUCK-IT!" MODE

HESITATION AND TENTATIVENESS ARE AT THE HEART OF THE challenge for many athletes at all levels of sport. Worrying about how things are going to turn out, concerns about "getting it right," distractions regarding consequences of certain in-practice or in-competition actions—these are just a small sample of the types of situations and thoughts that influence athlete behaviors.

When facing moments of indecision or anxiety or self-doubt, I have had a lot of success with this strategy: Literally say, "Fuck it!" and go "all in" on the decision and the action. "Fuck it!" doesn't mean "I don't care"—it means I accept the consequences and am going to stop worrying about how it's going to turn out.

Once there has been adequate deliberation on a game plan or on how to approach the next point or pitch, or even when the next technical or tactical adjustment feels scary or uncomfortable, "Fuck it!" seems to work for a fair number of athletes. **Athletes communicate that this strategy leads to feeling freed up and willing to take the risk that often aligns with effective execution.**

For years I have been asked whether or not I was going to write a book. I had several hesitations, one of them being the concern that I could not fully disclose and be authentic about how I *really* speak with and to athletes. I worried about offending readers with the type of language that exists in a locker room or clubhouse, which is often not on display for public consumption. But once I decided to write *One Day Better*, I knew I would only be satisfied with it if I chose to be transparent and authentic. So here I am modeling what I teach. I said, "Fuck it! I'm going all in with my full commitment to authentic language."

And here's a concession for those who might not prefer to say the F-word: "Screw it," "Do it," or a simple "I'm going all in on it" are all viable substitutes.

75

COURAGEOUS, NOT FEARLESS

AMONG THE OVERUSED WORDS IN SPORT'S CLICHED MOTIVATIONAL phrases is the concept of being *fearless*. T-shirts, posters, memes, and tattoos are rife with this word. And yet I've never met an athlete who was completely fearless. A complete absence of fear implies some sort of physiological or psychological pathology. Some level of fear exists inside every reasonably healthy human being on earth, though here I will not attempt to explain the biological and evolutionary imperative of fear being present in nearly all living creatures.

Here's where I agree with the notion of being "fearless": It is possible to get enough confidence, build enough wisdom or experience, or have a proper perspective on things so that you have a greatly reduced chance of allowing fear to influence your internal environment.

However, nearly every great athlete with whom I've worked—even those who were the most successful at the highest level in the world—has some level of fear about some element of their sport experience. **My emphasis with athletes is not to train for fearlessness; instead, we train for courageous or brave action when facing a situation where fear is present.**

I certainly advocate working to reduce fear and have guided many athletes to be more effective in fear management, but I also have dealt with my share of athletes who are distracted and upset because, despite all their best efforts, they still feel fear in some training or competitive situation. I think it is healthy for athletes to normalize fear, and I help them understand that what they're experiencing inside are essentially the sorts of feelings that nearly all athletes who have invested themselves in their sport have experienced at one time or another.

Each sport has its own unique manifestation of courageous action. For a golfer or tennis player, it may be swinging through the ball with full authority. For a baseball or softball pitcher, it might be delivering the pitch with aggressiveness. For a basketball, volleyball, or soccer athlete, it might be taking an assertive first offensive step rather than hesitating or freezing.

In every sport situation, there is an opportunity to exhibit brave and bold action that aligns with the task in front of you. Rather than worrying about being fearless, minimize your fear to the extent that you can, and act courageously to give yourself the best chance to be successful.

76

QUESTIONS TO ELIMINATE

IN SPENDING THOUSANDS OF HOURS OBSERVING AND CONSULTING with teams, watching coach–athlete interactions, and witnessing managers interact with employees, I've noticed how often communication breaks down. Too often, messages are not received in the way that the sender intended to deliver them.

There are hundreds of books written and entire educational courses designed to improve the quality and effectiveness of communication. It's my intention to guide you toward improved self-awareness so you can communicate more effectively, whether you are giving or receiving instruction.

I frequently see coaches deliver a message or make a point and then ask what appears to be a rhetorical question. Take your pick:

"Do you understand?"
"Does that make sense?"
"Everybody got it?"
"Are we all good?"
"Any questions?"

Nearly always, the athletes who are being spoken to will nod their heads as if they fully understand what was just said, implying that it completely makes sense to them. What I observe next is that the athletes frequently walk away and do not employ what was just taught or communicated.

Rhetorical questions lead to coach frustration, player confusion, execution breakdown, and an inordinate amount of time wasted circling back to communicating the exact same things a second or third time. As an example, I cannot count the number of times I've sat in on a time-out during a basketball or volleyball game and watched a coach design a play, asking, "Are we all on the same page?" only to see all the players look at each other with confusion as they head back out to the floor, where at least one player will completely miss their assignment.

There are two ways to approach these situations that will open up more effective, intentional communication.

First, I help the coach become aware of their tendency to follow up instruction with rhetorical questions, and I ask them to consider communicating differently. We work collaboratively to discern what might be a more effective way to communicate. Rather than ask, "Any questions?" it can be more productive to say, "What questions do you have?" This implies to the athlete that there are questions to be asked, and such a simple adjustment can immediately increase the frequency of questions of clarification. Another possibility after delivering instructions is to build a habit of asking any of the individual athletes to repeat or paraphrase what was just communicated. This keeps most of the athletes on their toes (because they don't want to be seen as inattentive or "getting it wrong") and reduces inaccurate communication.

Second, I have a conversation with all coaches and players in attendance to help them appreciate that these questions at the end of instruction are not rhetorical and that it is up to the players to ask questions of clarification anytime they are confused or feel they need additional information. This builds a culture of "safety" around asking questions and has the strong potential to improve the flow of information. When athletes get in the habit of asking clarifying questions, a shared understanding can be achieved more quickly.

77

MENTAL TRAINING VS. EDUCATION

WHEN I FIRST ENTERED THIS BUSINESS, I DEFINED WHAT I DID as *mental training*. Over the years, I've come to appreciate that my contribution is more accurately described as *mental education*. Why does this matter, and what are the implications of this distinction?

Far too many people who undertake the process of skill-building in this domain are anticipating some sort of "Aha!" epiphany after talking about or reading something related to mental skills development. People are inadvertently looking for a "tip" they can employ that could ostensibly hack their mental game and generate an immediate impact on their sport experience.

While there have been a number of occasions when I've worked with athletes and they've made some shocking improvements after our initial session, far more frequently, the slow trickle of our education and teaching sessions comes to fruition only after they have deliberately employed considerable reps in practice and competition.

Just like learning technical or mechanical sport skills or building physical strength, flexibility, or mobility in the gym, one can be exposed to principles that are very beneficial, but it is the consistent application of repetitions that develop the desired body or mind. I tell my clients, "I am here to work alongside you as we both engage in education and teaching, but you are wholly responsible for the training part." After all, a strength and conditioning coach can teach you proper lifting technique, but unless you're in the gym regularly working and applying that information, you will never get stronger.

The process of education is a crucial foundation that provides exposure and insight, but it has to be paired with ongoing and necessary application throughout the training process. There is no shortcut to any goal or destination worth arriving at. Learn a little, go do some work, learn from that, and repeat the process!

78

CHECK TEMPO AND MUSCLE TENSION **UNDER STRESS**

THERE ARE MANY PSYCHOLOGICAL AND PHYSIOLOGICAL CHANGES you can experience when you are under stress. Much of the feedback I give to athletes around their productive responses to stress is focused on thought process and attentional awareness. This includes a quick self-examination of the potential effect of stress on muscle tension and/or its impact on tempo or rhythm.

In regard to muscle tension, most all of us have natural, habitual tendencies to tighten up and store our stress with some regularity in the same parts of our body. Some people can identify the familiar tightness, while for others it takes intentional effort to increase their self-awareness so they can combat the effects of taut muscles. For some athletes, the tightness resides in their shoulders, while others clench their jaw and feel tension in their facial muscles. Some manifest their stress in their forearms, or hands, or legs. It is extremely beneficial to create a heightened awareness of how physical tension shows up in your body when you are in challenging situations. **Once you identify your proclivity, you can integrate short but effective techniques to minimize the effects of the tension and/or set yourself back to a less tense baseline.** This will allow for more fluidity of movement and a higher likelihood of a well-executed task. Even if your mind is not in the best place, with your body's tension minimized, you have a greater chance for success in that task. Some of these techniques you can use include:

- simple tense-and-release exercises
- a quick progressive-relaxation technique
- shaking out the tension from your body

Generally, all of these methods are enhanced with a practiced breathing technique to increase the likelihood of driving down the effects of the tension. Practice a variety of "antidotes" to determine which one will work most effectively for you.

In regard to tempo under stress, many athletes have a tendency to either slow down their natural rhythm or speed up their tempo. They will describe this disruption as a "guided" or "jabby" or "rushed" feeling that generally aligns with decreased or increased speed of movement. Quite often, athletes report that they were unaware that their tempo had changed until it was "too late." A quick self-check on the quality and consistency of your tempo, paired with a remedy to adjust back to optimal rhythm, will lead to better stress management.

Identify your tempo tendencies and work to get back on pace with the strategy that works best for you:

1. Practice intentional "slow-down" techniques, such as walking slower or taking more time between tasks.
2. Commit to rehearsing "back-to-rhythm" techniques, such as feeling real-time tempo in rehearsal/practice swings or reps, pacing up with walking, or having a quick cue to get back on task more efficiently.

You may not fully eliminate the stress, but you can raise your awareness around it and practice more effective ways of managing its effects on tension, tempo, and performance.

79

POST-EXECUTION DISCIPLINE IS JUST AS IMPORTANT

BOOKS AND PODCASTS ON MENTAL TRAINING FREQUENTLY mention the value of a pre-shot, pre-point, pre-pitch, or pre-execution routine. Being consistent in how you mentally approach each individual task within your sport has tremendous merit and has proven to be hugely beneficial to the athletes with whom I've worked.

On the other hand, what is far less often discussed is the additional value and benefit from an intentional and consistent post-shot, post-point, post-pitch, or post-execution routine. Having a clear plan about how you will consistently respond physically, verbally, and emotionally to situations can be extraordinarily helpful. Obviously, every circumstance has its own unique qualities. However, some structure around how you will manage those post-execution moments can help you reset and reorient, effectively "flushing" the previous moment and approaching the next moment with as little leftover residue as possible. Let's consider the different responses.

Physical response: A tennis player might turn their back to the net and walk away from the court for a few steps to disconnect from the previous point. They might also be intentional about keeping their eyes on the horizon rather than looking down, or they might use a focal point such as the strings on their racket to minimize external distractions. A golfer might take a rehearsal swing post-shot if they didn't like the way the previous one felt or momentarily close their eyes to anchor the feel of the previous swing if they liked the way the last one felt. A baseball or softball pitcher might swipe the dirt with their spikes after each pitch thrown to "draw a line" between pitches and get centered for the next one.

Verbal response: It is exceedingly helpful to be disciplined in how you speak to yourself after each task. What works best for an athlete is highly individualized, and determining what works most effectively for you is a significant step in your athletic development. One of my favorite suggestions is for the athlete to ask after each task, "What did I just learn?" This prompt underscores the value of seeking wisdom and the potential application of that knowledge at the next opportunity. In processing what just happened, use language that is productive and solution-oriented and as nonjudgmental as you can muster. I also strongly advise that your language quickly shift from what was just experienced to "next time" verbalization:

> "Next time, pay more attention to the wind."
> "Next time, get your feet to the ball more quickly."
> "Next time, see if you can feel that same feeling in your body—that worked great!"

The emotional post-execution response nearly always follows either the physical or verbal—or both. If an athlete does a great job of consistent application of physical and verbal post-execution strategies, quite often it does the trick to stabilize the emotional ups and downs that many athletes experience.

80

POST-EXECUTION GRADING

ONE OF THE SPECIFIC STRATEGIES THAT SEEMS TO WORK quite nicely for some is the tactic of giving oneself a specific "grade" after each execution. This concept is found in many mental training and sport psychology books, and it has a place in helping the athlete to focus on one shot, one point, one play, one possession at a time.

Implementing this strategy will vary depending on the pace of the sport. In golf, because of the amount of time between most shots, it's possible to reflect on the previous shot or internal environment (or whatever is being observed) and evaluate it. Generally, it is on a Likert scale of 1–4, given descriptions like "great," "good," "good enough," or "poor."

Hundreds of golfers whom I've introduced to this concept have invariably given feedback that they come to notice they hit far more "good enough" shots and fewer "poor" shots than they historically had been aware of. Left to their own evaluation criteria, most athletes are very harsh graders of themselves and often see things as binary—that shot was good, those shots were bad. **Reframing in a way that allows for more latitude and acceptance of shots that are, indeed, "good enough" keeps the individual from inaccurately interpreting**

how "poorly" they're playing. Over time, they begin to appreciate that they hit more "good enough" (or better) shots than they imagined.

In other sports, which may not have the luxury of such reflection in between points or pitches, there are often moments where action is paused momentarily. During these moments, it can be helpful for an athlete to simply "check-in" with regularity to make sure they are in a stable place with how they're evaluating themselves. This is also a good opportunity for them to work on regulating their language or breath or take other actions to bring themselves as close to neutral as possible.

This concept can also be applied more broadly—a "poor" training session where you didn't hit your power numbers or fully achieve the objective can become a "good enough" training session with context. For example, a triathlete understands that her 100 percent effort in that session was all that she could control and was quite likely additive to her fitness and developmental process. A "poor run" for a rodeo tie-down roper can be reframed as "good enough" given they drew a calf that hesitated out of the chute, which led to a less-than-optimal opportunity. A volleyball player can recognize that a serve hit with less-than-perfect precision and speed could still initiate a point that is won.

One caveat about this strategy: I am *not* suggesting that an athlete constantly evaluate their performance, asking questions like, "How am I doing today?" In fact, this is one of the greatest distractions that pulls athletes out of a state of "flow." The suggestions above simply provide the athlete with an opportunity to notice and then set the information aside as post-game, post-round, and post-competition data that can be utilized helpfully. If grading or noticing post-execution leads to overanalysis during performance, then this strategy may not be effective for you.

For many athletes, however, post-execution evaluation feels helpful and impactful in relation to their big-picture awareness that what they are doing is very often "good" or "good enough," which in turn feeds confidence and belief.

81

WE SEE THE WORLD NOT AS IT IS BUT **AS WE ARE**

THIS FAMOUS QUOTE HAS BEEN ATTRIBUTED TO MULTIPLE sources, including Anaïs Nin, Immanuel Kant, and Stephen Covey. Determining the originator of this idea, however, is far less important than applying the insight one can glean from it.

Every human on this earth is unique. No two people have ever experienced exactly the same things throughout their lives. Thus, each person has their own perceptions and biases through which they view and interpret the world.

It's good to appreciate that how you view things is only one way to see the world and that there are others around you who may see the exact same things differently than you do. **Once you deeply understand and appreciate this truth, you have the opportunity to reduce judgment of other people's tendencies, perspectives, or opinions.** When you can be less bothered by the perspectives of a teammate or a coach or a business colleague, empathy increases and you begin to move toward understanding. This can be hugely valuable when coaches are dealing with athletes, athletes are dealing with coaches, participants are dealing with officials, etc. There are an inordinate number of opportunities to apply this concept on a daily basis.

By appreciating that we all have our own views on things, not always trying to be right can help minimize tension, misinterpretations, and judgments that crop up in sport or life.

A little grace extended to others can go a long way toward creating an internal environment that is less distracted and consumed by differences of opinion. It affords us more space and energy for things that are within our control and move us further along on our pathway. In what situations do you have a tendency to be judgmental of others? How might you benefit from a change in perspective?

82

BE ALL THAT YOU **WANT TO BE** VS. ALL THAT YOU CAN BE

THERE IS AN IMPORTANT AND INTERESTING DISTINCTION TO be made between being "all that you can be" and "all that you want to be." I know that not everyone is in agreement with me on this, but I am a firm believer that every athlete has the right to determine their own criteria for success and to set their own agenda in regard to what they want to achieve and why.

For decades, I've worked alongside athletes who have received messaging that they *must* realize their potential, they *have to* maximize their God-given talent, and they *owe it to themselves* to be the best that they can be. This input frequently gets spun in the athlete's head as something that they *should* be doing or *need* to do, and they lose sight of whether they actually *want* to do it. In trying to satisfy the plans of their family, coaches, or community members, they can lose sight of their own reasons for participating in their sport, and this can have a damaging effect on motivation, passion, and determination.

This is a difficult concept for some parents to adopt and accept. They are aghast when their child says they may not want to play their sport in college or may not want to play professionally. On occasion, I get feedback that a parent believes their child needs some pushing in order to stay fully engaged—without the parents' persistence, the child might not be willing to do the work to achieve what they are capable of achieving. I never disagree with this sentiment. My response to the parents is that it might take pushing from others to get their child to achieve what is possible, but what is the potential cost involved in doing so? More times than not, I see this dynamic create parent–child conflict and become a relational issue in the household. Furthermore, it often costs the young athlete some of their own intrinsic pleasure of working on what they find interesting or challenging.

What I have found is that it can be very useful to guide the athlete toward an honest, transparent examination of their reasons for participating in and working at their craft. This often requires multiple discussions, as most of us have a difficult time determining whether our reasons are actually truly *our* reasons or whether we've just taken on the motives of others around us. This is a challenge for athletes of all ages.

Many times, once an athlete becomes accepting and comfortable with what they *actually want* from the sport, they approach their developmental process with less stress and more enthusiasm. It generates more internal desire and mitigates externally imposed pressure. What frequently transpires is additional desire for achievement based on their own criteria.

What do you want from your experience? Your answer is satisfactory as long as you're being honest with yourself. Honor your own desires and wants in relation to whatever you're hoping to accomplish.

83

RAFFLE TICKETS

HAVE YOU EVER PURCHASED A RAFFLE TICKET IN THE HOPES of having your number drawn so you can win the prize? On many occasions, it's been the case that I purchased many more tickets than the person who ultimately had their number drawn. It begs the question, "How did that person win with only 5 tickets when I bought 100?"

It is important to remember that having more raffle tickets in hand increases your odds, but it does not guarantee anything. This analogy is one I use often, but what does it have to do with sports or life?

The fact that an athlete has worked hard, put in the time, and made the investment or the sacrifice does not necessarily mean they will win their next competition or even have a more successful outcome than whatever happened previously. I encourage athletes to rest well, knowing that the more raffle tickets they have in their pocket—earned with every day of intentional work—the more likely they are to be successful. Give me 100 competition days, and the athlete who has accumulated more tickets is much more likely to win or be successful throughout those 100 days than the athlete who has fewer tickets. On a one-off day or week, the one with fewer tickets might be more successful, but over the long haul, the athlete who has done the work and banked progress will win their fair share.

The athletes I've worked with cite this as an extremely helpful concept because it directs them to work to increase their odds rather than looking to their practice/training/development as deserving some sort of immediate reward or prize. It also helps an athlete reconcile the emotional challenge of seeing a competitor or a teammate get the win or get the spot in the starting lineup despite that other person having done less work or having less investment or less commitment. Athletes are regularly distracted when they feel they have been beaten by someone who they believe has done less to *deserve it.*

Stay focused on putting a ticket in your pocket daily with a firm understanding that this is key to long-term success, and you can avoid ruminating over the short-term losses you may experience, while buying into the larger bet on your long-term growth and eventual success.

84

ACCUMULATED EVIDENCE

NATURALLY, CONFIDENCE AND BELIEF ARE CENTRAL THEMES in my discussions with teams, coaches, and athletes. Each individual person is unique in how they become successful in garnering belief and fostering confidence.

One of the common denominators I have witnessed among athletes with difficult-to-shake belief and confidence is an intentional method of accumulating evidence.

Gathering evidence typically entails keeping a journal, notebook, or diary of some sort that chronicles day-to-day preparation, competition, and rest days. Some athletes will watch film or video clips of their previous practices or contests. For others, evidence includes historical imagery exercises that refresh and replay earlier training moments or competitive successes. Still other athletes collect quotes or feedback from coaches, teammates, opponents, or fans that they can read and absorb or use as a reminder.

Our minds have a tendency to store negative experiences more easily and more permanently than positive ones. Fortunately, we do generally store memories of "big" moments when we have successes. However, not as easily or frequently logged are the reminders of the literally thousands of reps accumulated between preparation and competitions in which we did well or well enough.

Be diligent about having a way to remind yourself that you've done the work, that you've gathered the experience, that you've gained the wisdom. These points of evidence can be tremendous counterarguments to the self-doubt that nearly all of us allow to creep into our minds.

When you find yourself in a challenging moment and you wonder if you're good enough, if you're capable of succeeding, if you *have what it takes*, your ability to access valid accumulated evidence can be the difference between success and failure.

85

USE OPPORTUNITIES TO **NARROW ATTENTION**

BEING ABLE TO DIRECT AND SHIFT YOUR ATTENTION TO THE most productive place at the most productive time is critical to developing consistency in performance. Knowing when to shift attention is also of high value.

In closed sports that have a discernible pause in execution as a part of the game (e.g., golf between shots, baseball and softball between pitches, volleyball and tennis between points, gymnastics and diving between routines, etc.), it can be very helpful to use these brief pauses as an opportunity to reset one's attention on something that is constant and useful. While there are many options for where to direct one's attention available to the athlete, my first recommendation is that they try putting their attention on something tactical. Just before the pitch, serve, or shot, if the athlete has high clarity and intention around their tactics for the next pitch, serve, or shot, there is a likelihood that they can fill their minds with a productive and intentional strategy, thereby decreasing the chance of being distracted by other things.

Athletes regularly ask me about how they can stop thinking about something that is nonproductive—a bad shot, their poor execution on the last shot, worry about failing, etc. I redirect the question because it is not about stopping "bad" thoughts from popping in as much as it is about being disciplined in directing attention to a more helpful place, which reduces room in the brain for "bad" thoughts. **If the athlete develops a habit of knowing when they direct their attention (just pre-execution) and where they direct their attention (tactics), this can create a highly disciplined internal environment** which can facilitate more stability for the mind throughout training or competition.

Similarly, in an open sport that does not have consistent pauses (i.e., soccer, ice or field hockey, lacrosse, etc.) this method can be employed during momentary pauses in action (when the ball is out of play, immediately after a goal is scored, etc.). If these athletes get in the habit of reregulating their internal attentional space whenever there is a down moment in the game, it can be extremely useful. As well, even when the game is still "on," if a soccer player finds themselves distracted away from the most relevant things, reattaching to tactics is nearly always a helpful strategy. In soccer, this might be getting back to frequent head checks to see the spacing of the players on the field around them and then repositioning themselves in a way that fits the intended tactics of the moment.

Whatever sport you play or whatever endeavor you're hoping to be successful in, redirecting your attention to the tactical or strategic elements of what you're hoping to accomplish can be very useful.

86

HOW TO SPOT A TOXIC RELATIONSHIP WITH SPORT

WHEN I AM GETTING ACQUAINTED WITH A NEW CLIENT, I WILL ask, "What is your relationship with your sport?" I generally preface this question by saying I know it is a weird question, but the athlete's answer reveals valuable details that will assist me in guiding them toward greater success.

As with relationships between people, an athlete's relationship with their sport can be placed on a wide spectrum. Generally speaking, it's likely to be a complicated relationship, as is true with most relationships.

The level of "toxicity" in an athlete's relationship with their sport merits attention. When we discover unhealthiness in the relationship, it is time to go to work to repair damage and seek a more healthy or productive association.

For a number of my clients who are relationally challenged by their sport, it started because their introduction to the sport was through a parent or family member, and the sport became the parent's "thing" while the child never really learned to love it. These situations essentially function like an arranged marriage. Alternatively, there are times when I hear from athletes that their sport is the only thing they really talk about with one or both of their parents. Often it becomes, in the athlete's mind, the "thing" that largely defines their connection with their parent. When things go well on a given day in the athletic arena, all is well at home. When things don't go well, it puts negative interactions and/or relational tension into play.

For others, their toxic relationship is extensively generated and contained within themselves. How they perform in their daily interaction with their sport can have a tremendous impact on how the athlete feels about themselves on that day. A good day at practice translates to *I feel good about myself*, and a bad day at practice means *I feel poorly about myself*.

One of the essential steps in moving toward a healthy perspective is being willing to be honest with yourself about why you're involved in sport.

> What feels "at stake" when you're engaged in sport?
> How much have you tied your self-worth or your relational approval to the quality of your performances?

Deeply examining these types of questions can help you pursue a quest of alternative ways to interact with your sport and to intentionally substitute healthier thoughts and interpretations about the ways in which you choose to decipher your sport experience. Make sure to keep things in a healthy perspective.

While it's often difficult and nuanced, this work is incredibly impactful and rewarding for athletes.

87

BE YOUR BEST VS. BE THE BEST

THERE ARE SOME CIRCUMSTANCES WHERE PEOPLE USE LANGUAGE that sounds positive and constructive, yet it may generate an unhelpful effect on the person. One of these circumstances is when people share with me that they want to be "the best"—whether that means the best on their team, the best in the league, the best in their region, or the best in the world. Additionally, I hear coaches tell their athletes and teams things like:

> "We want to be the most hardworking team in the league."
> "We are going to be the best defensive team in the country."
> "You are going to be in the best condition of anyone in the competition."

Similarly, athletes will tell me they believe part of their confidence lies in showing up to competitions knowing they "trained harder than anyone there" or "made more of an investment/sacrifice than anyone at the race."

Initially, this language may feel to the athlete like motivation and inspiration; however, it often generates a comparative element

that I work hard to assist the athlete in disengaging from. As soon as anything comes into play where the goal is to be "better than them," it immediately puts some emphasis on what *they* are doing or how *they* are acting or what sort of work *they* have done. First, whatever "they" have done is completely out of your control. Second, how do you actually know what they have done? Is it actually more or less than you? How do you define "the best in the league"? Based on what parameters? Is it a fair and accurate and objective assessment?

In spite of the good intentions behind being "the best," my strong preference is to guide athletes toward being *their* best. The work you put in toward your own growth and development is completely within your control. The effort and intention and focus and dedication for you to be a master of your craft is your choice alone. I redirect athletes and teams toward doing their best to actualize their own unrealized potential if that's what they're striving for—and that is independent of anyone else in the world and has undefined limits and "upsides" that I want athletes and teams to work to discover.

I acknowledge that at times, seeing how others do things can give us information about how we might do something more effectively. If we keep our observations in that context, there doesn't have to be any comparative "better than" or "worse than" about it. But we all know that this is extremely difficult to do, which is why I strongly advise that when athletes show up to a competitive venue, they minimize how much they watch their opponents. If the athlete is "sizing up" their competition, they often see someone who looks more fit, or hits the ball farther in their warm-up, or seems supremely confident. This often triggers a cavalcade of thoughts that can lead to insecurity or self-doubt.

Certainly, the opposite can also be a challenge when an athlete finds their competition initially underwhelming and doesn't afford them appropriate credit. The end result might reflect their oversight, leading to post-competition comments like:

> "I can't believe she beat me; she looked terrible in her warm-up."
> "How do we lose to that team that looked so bad on film all week"?

There is certainly nothing inherently wrong in the message about being "the best," but I want to keep people directed toward the things they can control. Measure yourself against your own metrics and the metrics that your sport, or craft, or job demands. Any side glance to what others are doing as a way to measure yourself is a distraction from focusing on doing your own job.

88

THE SYSTEM MATTERS MORE THAN THE END GOAL

IN HIS BESTSELLING BOOK *ATOMIC HABITS*, JAMES CLEAR hits the bullseye with this statement: "Goals are for people who care about winning once. Systems are for people who care about winning repeatedly."

You will want to have clearly defined plans in place for the entire preparation phase, the lead-up to competition, immediately pre-performance, during the competition itself, and post-competition if you want to give yourself the best chance of being consistently competitive.

Far too many athletes in every sport and at every level allow some of these elements to be aimless, randomized, and even based on how they are feeling or thinking in a given situation. Great players take an intentional breath before *every* tennis serve, not just the ones that feel "big" or "important." Great athletes use a foam roller after their training *every* time, not just on the days when they feel like it or if their body feels sore. Great golfers adjust their internal language between *every* shot on the golf course rather than just when they're feeling underconfident or experiencing pressure.

Great athletes, coaches, and teams have real clarity about the goal(s) they'd like to achieve, and then they get down to the business of being locked in on and attentive to the tangible day-to-day or hour-to-hour or minute-to-minute actions that can be repeated. This is likely to include a disciplined system for sleep, nutrition, training, pre-hab/recovery, and routines (e.g., pregame, pre-point, pre-shot). When these systems become habitual, the athlete increases their chance of success.

It's the consistency of your input that gives you the best chance to deliver consistency in output. Intentional work to identify and then apply the systems and habits that help you get the most out of your training sessions, the most out of your competitions, and the most out of your life will pay dividends and help guide your mind and body to the most consistently effective place in the long run.

89

PRIORITIZE DECISIVENESS

THERE ARE PLENTY OF MOMENTS IN SPORT, BUSINESS, AND life when we hesitate to make decisions because we worry about getting it wrong or we want to make sure we get it right. Some people have the opposite issue around acting impulsively or not adequately thinking through their choices, but in the context of sport, I've encountered more athletes who are likely to be tentative and cautious—and fewer athletes who are likely to be impulsive—in both training and competition settings.

One of the ways that I guide athletes toward building habits of assertiveness and decisiveness is by encouraging them to have clear intentionality around valuing decisiveness over getting it "right." I will ask the tennis player, soccer player, golfer, triathlete, gymnast, etc. to execute their skill with their No. 1 priority being execution with decisiveness. When an athlete performs decisively and values their decisiveness, there is more acceptance of the outcome of that repetition. Going forward, they can put more "energy" toward measuring success based on making each decision in a timely and emphatic manner. Some of the inflection points that regularly occur in sport include:

- Pass or shoot the ball.
- Hit this tennis ball down the line or cross-court.
- Stay on the wheel of the rider who just passed you or allow them to gap you.
- Hit this golf shot with a hard 8-iron or a softer 7-iron.
- Choose this wave or wait for another.

Prioritizing decisiveness can assist the athlete in being "all in" in these moments.

In any of these instances, how the athlete evaluates these moments if the outcome is not what they desired is also critical. If they decisively pass the ball and happen to turn it over, do they then validate that at least they were being decisive, or do they simply emphasize the outcome failure, thereby reducing the likelihood that they will be decisive on the next rep? This is a crucial moment, because athletes who are willing to suffer some short-term pain in their outcomes—so that they can build decisiveness as a strength—will benefit from this approach. Those who shrink back in hesitation because of some short-term failures will deny themselves the long-term benefits of increased decisiveness. I remind athletes to make sure they don't change the rules of the game by going in with decisiveness as their prioritized intention, but then evaluate themselves exclusively based on outcome.

While I am never going to put a smiley face on a failed outcome, what I do want is for athletes to be willing to risk potential short-term sacrifices in terms of outcome so they generate more decisiveness. Sometimes an athlete might choose decisiveness in a practice or training session, but not yet in a competitive setting. This works well for some, as the consequences of a failed outcome are less consequential, and thus often easier to "risk."

Whatever method works for you, make sure that you continuously improve your decisiveness and employ less hesitation in order to take advantage of any of the opportunities you earn!

90

LOSE YOURSELF TO **FIND YOURSELF**

WHILE THIS CONCEPT CAN SEEM ESOTERIC, I'VE SEEN ATHLETES who can use it to their advantage, so let's explore the possibility.

Deep engagement in your sport or life experiences can sometimes make you feel like you are "lost" in the experience. This type of "flow" state—where you are immersed in honing a skill, learning new techniques, or executing well in competition—can sometimes feel disorienting relative to time and space. People speak of time slowing down or things seeming to go by quickly. Others recount how they sort of "blanked out" and forgot where they were for an instant because their focus was so intent on absorbing and/or appreciating the moment they were in.

Many people describe these moments to me as "finding themselves" or finding deeper clarity of purpose or meaning through their experience.

Sadly, a great number of athletes go through the motions of their sport at times, without a purposeful or deep sense of connection to their craft. They find themselves caught up in self-judgment and stressing about their performance or outcomes, by which point they are far removed from why they got involved in their sport or experience in the first place. I have seen far too many athletes deny themselves enjoyment in their sport experience because they were so wrapped up in performing well or performing poorly that they detached from the basic elements of the sport that initially drew them to choose their sport in the first place.

Allow yourself to engage in your sport as a craft. Cultivate a personal connection to how you practice it each day. **Revisit the mindset that first attracted you to your sport or craft so that you can remember why you fell in love with this experience in the first place.** I speak of it as honoring the little boy or girl who was first introduced to their sport.

You cannot cue a flow state, but when these fleeting moments happen to you, make sure that you absorb the experience and let yourself appreciate the lesson available to you.

91

FEAR REGRET MORE THAN FAILURE OR DISCOMFORT

FEAR OF FAILURE IS A CHALLENGE FOR MOST OF US. IT CAN interfere with the process and development of skills, the execution in training or competition, and/or the willingness to persevere, endure, and push through difficulties, at which point we find ourselves past the tipping point. This topic is in high circulation in my work with both athlete and non-athlete clients.

Another significant inhibitor specific to sports is that physical discomfort is necessary in order to prepare, train, and compete at the desired levels. Seeking out physical discomfort does not come easily to the general population, and even among many aspiring and accomplished athletes, it is often consciously or unconsciously avoided. If we broaden discomfort to include psychological, mental, or relational discomfort, it's possible to see that avoiding these experiences, either intentionally or unintentionally, can be a deterrent to the pursuit of excellence on one's journey.

One of the ways I frame this for anyone who aspires to improve themselves or to pursue ongoing achievement is to have a conversation about how they felt following a training session, competition, or even an entire season that was not met with the success they had hoped for. Inevitably, there is a level of regret expressed for not having pushed through fear or not having been willing to endure various types of discomfort in order to succeed. I leverage this awareness by suggesting, "Let's work to fear regret more than failure or discomfort."

Once an athlete, coach, or team identifies those moments that they have regretted and imagines moments in the future they want to manage less regretfully, we can begin talking about the requirements or decisions that can increase the likelihood for less future regret and more willingness to persevere in those moments that put them face-to-face with fear or discomfort.

What have you regretted about your past performances?
Next time you are faced with fear or discomfort, what specific choices or behaviors are you going to elicit in order to reduce your future regrets?

Embrace the idea that a desire to succeed and a willingness to act so you can reduce the potential for regrets is more important than what failure might cost. Invariably, even if you do "fail" or experience the intense discomfort of an activity, you will feel better about having done so and will likely walk away with fewer regrets because you understand that at least you were brave enough to give yourself a greater chance for success.

92

TAKE ADVANTAGE OF "WHAT IS"

BEING OBJECTIVE AND NEUTRAL ABOUT THE WAY SITUATIONS *are* versus how we would *prefer them to be* is an ongoing battle for many athletes and coaches. In virtually every sport and life circumstance, there are ideal conditions and there are innumerable variations that can be interpreted as less-than-ideal conditions.

Among the variations are weather; time delays; officiating competencies; the immediate health conditions of each individual; the quality of the field, venue, or race course; and so on. It's clear that this list and further iterations on these themes could be never-ending.

Those who give themselves the greatest chance for success take advantage of "what is" rather than wishing for things to be different. I want athletes to get clarity on "what is" and then get to task making the adjustments or adaptations necessary to accommodate those things that are happening right now.

- Is it starting to rain? How do you adjust what you're doing?
- The referee is calling fouls on seemingly insignificant contact? Modify your actions accordingly.

- Your teammate is slower today than normal? How can you assist or inspire them or adjust your own execution, taking this into account?
- The putting surface is faster than it was yesterday? How do you regulate your putting speed to best effect?

Once you are able to accept "what is," you can look for effective adjustments and solutions and minimize the distraction brought on by the desire for something to be different. It's yet another hallmark of the most successful athletes.

Having been tasked to do literally thousands of pregame, half-time, and night-before-the-event chats or speeches with teams and athletes, I often invoke "solution mode" as a nonnegotiable and something that is a mental discipline separator. Left to their initial reactions and emotions, athletes are far more likely to succumb to the increased anxiety that arises when the going gets tough. Solution mode is a valuable reminder to pivot away from the momentary distraction and seek an adaptation that assists in achieving success.

Make a choice to lock in on the immediate task, rather than being distracted by circumstances you would prefer. Ask yourself, *How do I take advantage of what is available to me right now?*

93

ELIMINATE VICTIM MENTALITY

HERE IS A SHORT NOTE REGARDING A PARTICULARLY UNHELPFUL mental habit that some of us fall into: responding to things as though we were victimized.

> "The referees have it out for us."
> "The other team got lucky."
> "I always start on the side of the court where the sun is in my eyes."
> "That's just my luck."

In writing this book, it's my intention to increase self-awareness so that you might make conscious choices about sustaining certain self-talk or being purposeful in changing it.

Check in with yourself. If your tendency and habit is to blame others and finger-point or see the world as against you, recognize that these are your own thoughts and not reality. Now, there certainly are times when things don't go our way and times when one might be legitimately victimized, but these are not the situations I'm addressing. I'm talking about the situations where we feel like the world owes us something or we're entitled to something and/or we should be getting sympathy from others.

Stop feeling sorry for yourself—no pity parties. **Work to change your thoughts so you can start taking ownership for what you were responsible for and what is in your control to change in a subsequent situation.** Move toward solutions and actionable steps that you can take.

Blaming others, making excuses, and acting victimized have no place in the world of elite performance.

94

WORK THE PUZZLE

AS AN AVID FAN OF BRAINTEASERS AND PUZZLES, I'VE COME to realize that the challenge of working relentlessly to "figure it out" is where the bulk of the enjoyment is found. Getting the solution is often satisfying, but the real joy is in the small revelations along the way that lead to a possible outcome.

I reference this concept with athletes and clients irrespective of the sport or job they are immersed in. Rather than being fixated on getting it right or not messing up or becoming upset by a short-term failure, I prefer the notion of seeing every moment in sport as one more clue toward eventually "solving the puzzle." Every shot a golfer takes, every forehand a tennis player hits, every mile a triathlete logs, every rep done by any athlete in practice or competition, is one more bit of feedback about what works or what doesn't work. It is helpful for athletes to see every moment as additive to their growth and development.

Many of my clients have appreciated the idea that solving a simple or easy puzzle is unsatisfying in the long run. Yes, occasionally it feels nice to have a puzzle that is very straightforward and requires little effort. But most agree that the real sense of satisfaction comes from selecting a difficult puzzle and working tirelessly to solve it. It's similar to an escape room—multiple clues are waiting to be discovered, each one guiding the participants toward success. Keep this in mind as you push through your frustration and confusion immediately following any attempt to "solve" your current challenge. If you stay patient with the process, the solutions will eventually become evident.

Sport, work, and life present very difficult puzzles. **See every moment as additive to your work toward a solution.** Increase your awareness that every obstacle presented is helpful in guiding you toward expertise.

95

DEVELOP A MINDSET THAT **MANAGES UNCERTAINTY** WELL

MANY YEARS AGO, I TOOK ADVANTAGE OF AN OPPORTUNITY TO see author and philosopher Sam Keen speak. Having read and been impacted by his books, I waited around after his talk to ask him for guidance on my tendency to worry about the future and whether I would "make it"—professionally, relationally, and personally. He smiled at me and said it sounded like I had a lot of work to do on my relationship with uncertainty, suggesting, "If you can work toward being at peace with uncertainty and accept that we have little control over things, you will move in the direction of 'making it.'"

I have taken his sage advice and shared elements of it with thousands of athletes over my career. I will admit that I am still poor at managing uncertainty well, but I have grown in my awareness of when it takes over my thoughts, and I work hard to cope with this when it occurs.

For many athletes, change is difficult. They know that what they are doing isn't working optimally, but to change requires a willingness to take the leap into an even more uncertain future:

Will this new technique work?
Will switching coaches actually help me get better?
Would attempting this new thing actually pay off?

The notion that "we tend to prefer the certainty of misery to the misery of uncertainty" holds true.

Uncertainty feels so miserable to some that they're willing to stay stuck in what they're doing, despite feedback that they are not achieving at their highest level. It requires courage and hard work to minimize concerns about getting it "wrong" and to be willing and brave enough to attempt intelligent and conscientious change.

Being "good" or "good enough" is the enemy of greatness. If you want to break through in whatever endeavor you're undertaking, it demands that you be willing to suffer some short-term uncertainty about your future in order to give yourself your best chance to be extraordinary.

96

FAIR BUT NOT EQUAL

THIS CONCEPT CAN BE A TOUGH SELL TO SOME ATHLETES. It proves particularly challenging in a group setting where teams, squads, or members are getting different levels of attention and/or seemingly distinctive opportunities from one another. Athletes share their observations about how *it isn't fair* —the coach treats some people more harshly or with more understanding. Or they express *it doesn't seem fair* that some teammates can make many mistakes before being removed from the lineup, while others make only one minor mistake and get removed.

They are misinterpreting unequal treatment as unfair treatment. **In the real world of high-level athletics, athletes are treated differently. They are not treated equally. This does not mean that it's unfair.**

It is fair that each athlete gets a chance to practice every day. It is fair that each has an opportunity to participate and show their skills and receive a fair chance to earn a role on the team. Once these decisions are made by the coaches, they typically may direct a disproportionate amount of their coaching time and energy to the athletes who are most likely to be in the competitions. Helping athletes reconcile this reality is crucial for them to refrain from interpreting this dynamic as "the coach is playing favorites" or "the coach doesn't care about me." Generally speaking, coaches work hard to care about everyone on their roster. They work to give everyone a chance and an opportunity, which is fair. From that point on, they often direct their primary energies toward the athletes who they perceive will give the team the best chance to win. This is the coach's job.

Next time you find yourself feeling treated "unfairly" by a coach or a manager, make sure that it is truly unfair—you didn't get *any* chance to earn a spot or didn't have *any* opportunity to make an impression? If this is not how it literally went down, could it instead be the case that your treatment was unequal? This is the stuff of high-level sports, and while it may be painful to be on the receiving end of such treatment, it is valuable to frame it in a way that is most accurate and then get back to the work of developing and improving your skills, which will enhance your chances of achieving your goals down the road.

97

PIZZA AND CHOCOLATE

I ONCE HEARD SOMEONE SAY, "I LOVE PIZZA AND CHOCOLATE. When they are good, they are amazing, and even when they are not very good, I still enjoy them." This got me thinking that this concept can be applied to our relationship with our sport or career or even our personal relationships.

If an athlete has deep passion for their sport, the fleeting and infrequent moments of success and "winning" feel amazing. The clarity of having gotten better at an element of their craft feels really good too.

For those who find joy and desire in what they are doing, it's also true that if the love and appeal run deep enough, after the initial sting that comes when things don't go so well, there is a sense of appreciation for having gone through the experience. Certainly, it doesn't taste *as good as* when things are going well, but there can still be a thankfulness for having given oneself the opportunity for a peak moment and for having felt the emotions of caring deeply for something—even if the momentary experience was somewhat painful.

If someone loves something or someone deeply enough, then it puts into play both the opportunity for deep joy and also the opportunity for deep disappointment or pain. Loving a certain type of food means that we learn to be okay when the food isn't completely up to our standards, and we keep seeking an improved experience with it. Similarly, if our temporary experience with our sport is underwhelming, plugging into the love we have for it—the essence of why we are working hard at this pursuit—can sometimes recalibrate our perspective on that disappointing moment.

Make a choice to savor remarkable moments. Also remember to be okay with those moments where things don't go exactly as you might prefer.

98

DO HARD THINGS

INVARIABLY, AT SOME POINT IN MY CONSULTATION WITH CLIENTS, they will say, "This is really hard!" My typical response to this is, "No shit!"

It is difficult to be great at anything. It is difficult to build technical skills. It is difficult to be nutritionally sound. It is difficult to train and condition one's body and push it to the edge without injury. The list of what is difficult or hard is almost endless.

There is a plethora of research evidence that has been collected to indicate that from a societal perspective, young people being raised in Western cultures in the past couple of decades have slowly become more inclined to believe that things *should* come easier. There is instant information in the devices they carry 24/7. Want to watch a movie? Start streaming it in minutes. Want to buy something? Go online and it will be delivered to your doorstep.

In addition, there are a greater number of young people today who have been denied the opportunity to "figure it out" on their own. There are parents who are overinvolved in their children's lives. Some of these children have tutors and private coaching for multiple aspects of their performance. There are answers for everything on Google or YouTube. This is not to say that these things are inherently bad or wrong.

It's been my experience that while some of these conveniences are valuable and helpful, they can also inhibit hands-on lessons on how to deal with adversity. There actually is a term that's been coined for this: *failure deprivation.*

What this creates for some people is the misperception that one can have nearly whatever one wants in some sort of shortcut fashion. However, this is certainly not the case when it comes to high performance in sport or any truly worthwhile endeavor.

Here's a strong message I relay to my clients: Expect things to be difficult, and expect them to take longer and to take more work than you realize. Be prepared to endure whatever it takes to give yourself a chance to manifest your potential and possibly reach your goals. **Be willing to do hard things, and don't for a second believe it should be easier.**

This mentality is grounded in reality and crucial for athletes as they encounter difficulties and persevere through obstacles and challenges.

99

NO END IN SIGHT

I SEE VALUE IN BEGINNING SOMETHING WITH AN END IN MIND. However, I have also seen tremendous accomplishments in sport flow out of beginning with an intention to discover what we find at the "end." Being willing to leave the end undefined can sometimes lead to greater possibilities.

The creative growth process for many athletes who have succeeded in multiple domains often comes from their living each day with an open mind, ready to explore and examine whatever that day's feedback presents. This can coexist alongside clear intention of what one hopes to achieve in a given training session or competition, but it allows for the opportunity to deliberately seek moments to adapt and flex based on what is happening in real time.

Constantly being prepared to scrutinize immediate feedback and being willing to go with what we're learning often allows athletes to "go to places" and reach developmental destinations they had not even dreamed could be feasible.

Rather than a mindset of "I don't think that will work" or "That's not relevant to the pathway toward my goals," we are speaking about a mindset of:

"Let's see how we might learn something from this."
"Is it possible that this can help me build strengths I was unaware of?"
"I'm not sure how this might help me, but let's give it a try."

I believe there are fewer limitations in play if the endgame remains undecided and undefined. Growth, expansion, discovery, creativity, and acceptance become the goal, and "where this leads" is a secondary objective.

It takes tremendous fortitude and discipline to be willing to give over to the creative side and to be willing to embrace that growth in any direction could be a desired route. Expend some effort to see if you could be willing to incorporate this approach more in the work in which you engage. It is truly awe-inspiring what many people have discovered simply by letting themselves be open to the discovery process itself.

100

OWN YOUR ROLE ON THE TEAM

WHETHER INVOLVED IN A TEAM SPORT OR A GROUP AT WORK OR an assembly of people in any situation, one of the tests we all face is to get clarity about what our roles are within that group. A further challenge for all of us to work toward is acceptance of those roles—and an ownership of those roles once we are clear and accepting of them.

One of the most obvious applications of this concept comes in team sport settings. Athletes move up the ladder from their junior years into college settings, and sometimes then into professional settings. As this progression occurs, athletes frequently find themselves internally conflicted by the shifting of their role within their team. The high school "superstar" who was the captain of the team and the best in their region or state might suddenly find themselves as someone who rarely (if ever) gets playing time. This sort of role change occurs every year with every team, as the constellation of the team changes with athletes graduating or retiring or moving on for various reasons.

Early on in each unique group circumstance, do the work to define what your ascribed role is. Own that role with appreciation and enthusiasm. Every athlete gets "fed" primarily from playing time and success in their sport, but there are a plethora of contributions a player can make in or out of the game itself. **Seek opportunities to**

take advantage of those moments when you can make a contribution for the good of the group and for your own self-satisfaction. Owning, acknowledging, and embracing your role—whatever that may be—can generate the sense that "this is my house, this is my job, this is how I help us all move toward success."

Engage in those activities that align with your role and take pride in doing them to your utmost ability to reduce the likelihood that you are distracted by the role you *don't* have or the tasks that are *not yet* your responsibility.

101

SCARCITY VS. **ABUNDANCE**

HERE IS SOMETHING I HAVE OBSERVED IN VIRTUALLY EVERY SPORT: During a training session or in a warm-up prior to competition, an athlete will do something well. A basketball player will hit a difficult shot, a golfer will sink a long putt, a tennis player will smack a serve that would be impossible to return, a soccer player will bend a ball beautifully into the goal. However innocently and jokingly, I will then hear the athlete say to herself or to a teammate—or a coach or a well-intended parent will say something to the athlete—like, "There are only so many of those good ones, so don't waste them in practice/warm-up."

It stands to reason that if there is one of those "in there," there are more "in there" as well. **I want you to see well-executed moments from a perspective of abundance—knowing there are many more of these available to you.** I want you to acknowledge your skill set and ability to execute well. I want you to see these as possibilities that might happen again, rather than as luck or as scarce in availability.

Seeing good things happening as abundant rather than scarce is a choice and a habit that can be learned. This is not seeing things through a lens of *expecting* them to happen, but instead acknowledging that these good things *can* happen. And when they do occur, recognize that there are plenty more where those came from.

102

BEWARE OF INTERPRETATIONS

MISINTERPRETATIONS OF OTHER PEOPLE'S ACTIONS OR WORDS can lead to serious consequences. Throughout world history, multiple wars have been started based on miscommunication and misunderstandings that then escalated into bloodshed.

While considerably less consequential, I have witnessed hundreds of situations where a coach misinterprets an athlete's actions, an athlete misinterprets a coach's actions or words, or others within the developmental system around an athlete are misunderstood or misperceived.

It is hugely important that everyone in the system who is working collaboratively for the betterment of the athlete or team be willing to ask questions of clarification and/or be prepared to discuss any possible conflicts or concerns.

Left to their own interpretation of things, many people have a tendency to make assumptions that are at times inaccurate. These inaccurate assumptions then get communicated within a system, and this creates unnecessary turmoil and stress for all involved.

I have witnessed on several occasions highly talented teams be taken apart by miscommunication. Players within a team misperceiving their teammates' intentions can foster:

A sense of disloyalty: "They don't have my back."
A sense of distrust: "I don't think they care about anyone but themselves."
And/or disrespect: "Obviously, they don't care about the right things."

These perceptions can flow out of a completely inaccurate interpretation of someone's behaviors and quickly erode the foundational cohesiveness of a team.

Around individual sport athletes who have achieved at the highest levels (e.g., Olympic gold medals, No. 1 world rankings, national championships), I have seen the personnel within their "entourage" miscommunicate, which then leads to the downfall of the athlete's chances of success.

Work to get clarity of intention from the people with whom you interact because oftentimes the intention of a person's words or actions is not perceived accurately.

Asking questions can be uncomfortable and often requires courage:

"Can you help me clarify what you just said?"
"This is how I'm interpreting what you just did/said. Is that accurate?"
"I want to make sure I'm not misunderstanding you. Can you say that again?"

These questions, and others like them, can be game-changers that help keep the peace within the system so that all people in the athlete's "bubble" stay on the same page and are being heard and understood precisely and accurately.

103

CONTEMPLATION VS. ACTION

THERE IS A FASCINATING DYNAMIC AT WORK IN A MULTITUDE of situations in sport. Throughout the preparation phase, during pre-competition, while the competition is underway, and after the competition is completed, there is a continual back-and-forth between thinking and doing.

It is of great benefit for any of us to have insight into our tendencies in any or all of these situations. Some people are inclined to be contemplative and less action-oriented. Others have the opposite proclivity and will take action without much thought. The key is to strike the balance in knowing the times when contemplation and thinking are most helpful and beneficial and the times when being more reactive and reflexive with behaviors is warranted.

Those who become aware of their action taking precedence may find at times that their behaviors are impulsive and/or spontaneous without adequate information to make wise moves. Learning how to "take a moment" in these situations can be productive. The decision to change an in-game tactic or strategy based on just one moment of "failure" is an example of this. On the other hand, there may be moments where that sort of organic snap decision and action may be merited and effective.

Contrarily, for those who have a tendency to err on the side of contemplation, recognize that you might get "stuck" or slowed down because of overthinking or worrying about getting it wrong or making a mistake. This could be evidenced when an athlete doesn't make adjustments or adapt to seemingly obvious information. In these instances, it is helpful to learn to be more courageous or body- or action-based in order to "just do it." Contrarily, in other situations, being thoughtful can be what the job calls for, and that will guide you to make a thorough analysis, which leads to more efficient or effective action.

The essence here is to be more aware of your tendencies and attuned to what is functionally being asked of you in the immediate situation. **Matching contemplation and action appropriately to a given circumstance will help you be more successful in the task of the moment.**

104

YES MODE VS. MAYBE OR NO

MAKING SPLIT-SECOND DECISIONS IS AN INTEGRAL PART OF many athletic situations. Whether to swing at a pitch in softball, to move in or back in soccer, or to take the shot or pass in basketball are among the myriad real-time choices constantly facing an athlete.

My experience has been that many athletes find their willingness and clarity around such decisions becoming influenced, compromised, or hijacked. There's a litany of reasons why these decisions are sometimes less than optimal. Every individual, every situation, every moment, has its own subtleties and nuances.

However, one thing I've found helpful for many athletes in situations that demand quick decisions is learning how to be in what I refer to as "yes mode." In this internal environment, rather than reading the cues with "maybe" in mind—which then requires a yes or no decision—my recommendation is often to be committed to "yes" with full intention to act accordingly, until or unless the cues that are read create a "no."

Here are a couple of real-life examples that occur with frequency in my consultations: A baseball player deciding whether or not to swing at a pitch can attack a pitch with full intention if he's looking for a pitch on the inner half of the plate. If the pitch happens to be thrown there, he has been green-lighted, and he swings. If the pitch is thrown anywhere else, while he's prepared himself for an inside pitch, anything else becomes a red light, meaning "no swing." For those who know baseball intimately, there are circumstances where just looking for an inner half pitch is not warranted. However, in the instances in which this is true, this is far more effective than a "maybe" and also more effective than anticipating a yes/no decision.

A tennis player is on the baseline in a rally, but she is in "yes mode" in her mind, meaning she is prepared to step into the court and attack a short ball. Far too many times, a short ball will present itself and the player, who was in "maybe" mode, missed the opportunity because of the split-second indecision that flows out of an indecisive mindset. **"Yes" means anticipating the opportunity with every ball, and if it's there, recognizing and attacking happen instantly.** "Yes" means you still anticipate the opportunity, but if you quickly recognize it's not there, you shut down the attack for one more ball, and then anticipate it on the next one.

In so many sports, and in so many situations, the idea of being "all in" on a decision as a "yes," and then shutting it down if it doesn't present itself, keeps the athlete aggressive, sharp, and making quick decisions. Everything is a green light until it is not! Look for opportunities to apply "yes mode" in your training, in your competitions, and in your life.

105

SUFFICIENT VS. 100 PERCENT

ONE OF THE HALLMARKS OF MANY GREAT ATHLETES AND accomplished coaches is that they are constantly and consciously striving to get 100 percent out of every opportunity in which they find themselves. What is also true is that getting 100 percent out of an opportunity rarely happens.

I find it valuable to discuss the cost of extra energy expended relative to the incremental value of trying to squeeze out that last 1 or 2 percent in preparation or in a performance. When I engage athletes and coaches in this conversation, it can initially seem contrary to the mindset of pushing for 100 percent, so I'm met with raised eyebrows or other pushback from the client.

Of course, there is no hard-and-fast rule that applies to all situations. Certainly, there may be situations where, upon examination, the athlete or coach decides intentionally that going "all in" is warranted despite the potential consequences of burning up energy that could be used later. However, in my experience, there are other times where, upon examination, both the athlete and the coach feel as though more repetitions, more time practicing, or more effort expended is less valuable than allowing for more recovery time.

For example, when nearing the end of a long training block, it can be tempting to keep pushing hard through the last day or two of training. But it could also be that this final "push" actually puts the athlete or team over their threshold of being able to recover adequately for their next effort. Coming back the next day with fresh physical and emotional energy can often trigger a more effective and efficient progression in whatever skill one is trying to develop or hone.

Furthermore, from a psychological perspective, there are times where getting to "good enough" and then moving along can be more beneficial than striving for that last incremental bit. **There is a fine line between working relentlessly toward excellence and demonstrating unhealthy perfectionism.**

Having a solid work ethic and holding yourself to a high standard is clearly the hallmark of an elite athlete. Let's just make sure that the "extra mile" one might put in is not one that takes away from subsequent sessions or unnecessarily puts one at greater risk for injury. Do an honest evaluation about what is sufficient and truly necessary versus what is maximized or at 100 percent. Being clear about how and why to define the endgame of today's efforts can be an invaluable exercise and guide the athlete and coach toward more effective training and competitive goals.

106

DON'T CONFUSE ACTIVITY WITH **PROGRESS**

WHEN I'M CALLED IN TO WORK WITH A TEAM OR ORGANIZATION or am welcomed into the inner circle of an athlete's developmental "team," I first get my bearings by determining what is currently being done and gauging how effectively things have been working. Essentially, it is an audit of what is happening.

In a surprising number of situations, there is *a lot* going on and people appear to be very busy putting in the work, but progress has become stagnant, plateaued, or even regressed. When I initially offer feedback, I often hear about how hard everyone is working and the number of hours that are being dedicated to the task. There's a caution here: *Do not confuse activity with progress.* **Is the work you are putting in actually making things better, or is it just making things different?**

This means taking a hard look in the mirror for most of us, as we assume our sweat and blood translate into traction and movement toward our end goals. But working harder does not necessarily mean we're moving in a helpful direction. Here are some clear examples of this:

- An athlete overtrains and generates higher potential for injuries.

- Coaches overcoach and deny athletes an environment where they can be more instinctive and "organic."
- Team leaders micromanage their staff and stifle autonomy and creativity.

It is critically important to periodically check that you're going in your intended direction. Having honest and objective metrics to define your "progress" and the progress of your "team" will keep your effort effective and minimize wasted energy and time.

While you're working hard, it does not guarantee that you're going in a productive direction, or in any direction at all. Bring an open-mindedness and humility to checking in on your activities so you can be sure your efforts are fruitful and your perception of progress is objectively true and valid.

107

DEVELOP A HEALTHY PERSPECTIVE

ONE OF THE THINGS I'VE ATTEMPTED TO DO THROUGHOUT MY entire career is to bring a bit of levity and lightheartedness to situations. While those who have worked with me would acknowledge that I am serious about the work I do with my clients and am earnestly focused on their growth and development, many would also say I'm constantly teasing and making jokes and working to keep things "light." The older I get, the more I'm accused of making "dad jokes."

First, selfishly, this is the sort of work environment I prefer. Second, I strongly believe that **bringing humor into the serious business of athlete development helps keep things in a healthier perspective and presents a setting where judgment and criticism are reduced.**

This, of course, does not mean minimizing how someone is feeling in a situation or being free to mock or belittle or invalidate someone's own interpretations of their experience. Instead, it's better to help guide the person back to a more stable and rational place in their mind and in their viewpoint.

When I am observing an athlete in training, if they make a mistake, I might look at them with a smile on my face or say something like, "That's probably not going on your highlight film." A comment like this is frequently met with a laugh or reciprocal smile, as the athlete attaches less meaning to the situation and finds room for levity in a moment that really was not that important.

Any coach or athlete has the option to bring lightness or humor to their intense moments. In addition to this, seeing things in the broader context of life and looking at the daily challenges from a 30,000-foot viewpoint can help mitigate the momentary frustrations that are going to occur regularly in a competitive culture.

Work toward being more intentional about your mindset—deliberately keep things light, see the humor in most situations, and keep things in perspective.

108

WHO DO YOU WANT TO BE?

I HAVE REFERENCED QUOTATIONS FROM JAMES CLEAR'S BOOK *Atomic Habits* elsewhere in this book. Another of my favorites that I've used with multiple clients is the notion that "every action that you elicit is a vote for the person that you want to be."

Here's a series of questions that uses this idea to guide your development:

- What type of person/athlete/coach would you like to be?
- What are the characteristics, what are the principles, that reflect who you would like to be?
- What are the values that you would like to have reflected in your life?

Now, identify the types of actions and behaviors that align with these nonnegotiable principles.

Anywhere you find misalignment between what you say reflects your deepest intentions and what you are actually doing, there's an opportunity for discussion and adjustment. If you say you want to be a person who does *x* but instead you are doing *y*, then you are essentially casting a vote to be a *y* sort of person and are distancing yourself from the *x* person you claim you want to be.

Deep reflection on this misalignment can be challenging and eye-opening. In the end, it often comes down to a person either making the desired changes to align with their stated goals or facing the painful realization that while they say they want to be a particular way, they aren't willing to prioritize the actions that support this. My response in these situations is generally to propose that the person stop stating that making changes is important to them, because their words and their deeds are incongruent.

I use this concept in early season team meetings and with corporate teams. I ask the group to identify and define the values and characteristics that they would like to embody, along with the requisite behaviors. This exercise provides a helpful and highly effective blueprint to guide the team. If being a certain kind of person is of high value to you, then start working to become that person with consistent, daily actions.

109

ARE YOU WILLING TO SUFFER?

HAVING WORKED WITH VIRTUALLY TENS OF THOUSANDS OF athletes over my career in individual, group, and team settings, there are some common denominators that emerge which are shared by many athletes at all levels. One of those characteristics is that most people (even athletes) look to avoid discomfort and want things to be easier.

In my experience, the athletes who are willing to suffer—physical discomfort, environmental discomfort, mental and emotional discomfort—are the ones who give themselves the best chance to be elite. The best of the best are willing to push through those moments of strain and take themselves to the next levels of development and learning. They recognize that the temporary suffering is tied to a greater, long-term intention or dream or goal, and they embrace the challenge in fighting through their innate reaction to stop or slow down or throttle back in those moments.

Oftentimes people see the best athletes in the world achieving great things on their biggest stages—World Championships, the Olympic Games, National Championships, Grand Slams, the Majors—and they have not an inkling of the suffering these athletes have endured in order to hone their craft and have their skills hold up under the competitive pressure.

Parents regularly deny their children the opportunity to work through moments of discomfort by jumping in to make things easier. Coaches sometimes will be lax in providing training sessions that truly take their athletes to their edge. One of the challenges as a sports parent or a coach is to allow the athlete to push themselves to the edge and test their own resilience and fortitude. This denies the athlete the opportunity to explore and develop coping strategies.

Of course, there are, unfortunately, parents and coaches who create environments that are unhealthy and put athletes in positions where that extra push is actually harmful or detrimental to the athlete's health or well-being. That "fine line" is crossed when the parent or coach pushes or aggressively demands rather than guides or inspires or allows the athlete to figure it out for themselves.

For the athlete, it's important to know that some suffering is required in order to be great—it's not optional. Also know that **the push to achieve greatness has to come from within you—it can't be manipulated, controlled, or forced by anyone else.** Once you've decided that deep in your heart you are willing to do what is necessary to give yourself a chance for mastery, be ready to dig deep and suffer at times in order to give yourself the best chance to succeed.

110

CATCH YOURSELF AND OTHERS DOING THINGS WELL

ONE OF THE TASKS WITHIN A TEAM IS FOR THE COACH, CAPTAIN, or team leaders to hold people within the team accountable. Often in team discussions, this takes the form of the leaders keeping team members in line, being willing to "call them out" if things aren't being done in the fashion acceptable within the culture, essentially policing the rest of the team for what they might be doing wrong.

Generally, I will allow the team leaders to have their say, and then I will add, "Whose job is it to catch the team members doing things well?" My experience has been that the coaches and leaders of a team are far more likely to be listened to if they are not only addressing the things that are "bad," but they're also intentional about recognizing and acknowledging the things their teammates are doing well. End-of-practice shout-outs and acknowledgments and in-practice or competition feedback ("I see you working!" "Nice pass!" "You crushed that last set!") are examples of how **team leaders (and everyone else) can reinforce the types of actions that are aligned with the culture of excellence.**

Similarly, most athletes with whom I work are initially quite adept at catching themselves doing things poorly and are very critical of themselves when they err or fail. On the contrary, few athletes will reinforce reasonably successful moments or "pat themselves on the back" unless something very special happens. I encourage all with whom I work to appreciate the things they do—even what they think of as mundane. "Why would I give myself credit for that? It's what I'm supposed to do." Certainly, I'm not proposing you throw a party for yourself for any and all of the myriad things you do well in a training session or a competition. However, I do encourage a slow drip of a reminder about the "I do this every day" sorts of achievements. These small gains add up to excellence because they keep you accurately assessing your skills, filling your confidence up with acknowledgment of the investment you're making, and avoiding the tendency to exclusively emotionalize and emphasize the things you do "wrong."

Just as a teammate or leader can be more effective by appreciating what is going "right" as well as pointing out what is going "wrong," so can any athlete maintain more consistent confidence and a more stable internal environment by catching themselves doing things well.

111

ASK FOR INPUT WITH A BEGINNER'S MINDSET

WHEN IT COMES TO YOUR GROWTH AND DEVELOPMENT AND pursuing your goals, whom do you trust to give you quality feedback? One of the most invaluable aspects of a productive pathway to success is getting outside feedback that is helpful, timely, and accurate.

There are some who have a difficult time accepting feedback, and some who appear eager to get feedback from anyone with an opinion. Identifying the person or persons from whom you want to receive feedback and being willing to receive information and thoughtfully consider it is essential to maximizing your potential.

Work hard to remain curious with a beginner's mindset—*I don't know what I don't know.* Rather than getting angry, frustrated, or stubborn about receiving feedback, see it as something to ponder before outright rejecting it or taking it personally. Most beginners are eager to know how they can improve and recognize the opportunity in all feedback to help them develop. As athletes become more proficient and skilled, there are some who slowly begin to resist input from others, effectively shutting down some growth opportunities. Others continue to foster an attitude that anyone with whom they interact has the potential to teach them something new and helpful. This is certainly true of some of the best coaches in the world with whom I've interacted. I remember specifically sitting in a meeting in the '90s when David Leadbetter was coaching many high-profile golfers, including two who each rose to No. 1 in the world in their careers. A 20-year-old intern was present and commented on something, which David encouraged him to elaborate on. While this was happening, David was furiously scribbling notes about how he would leverage this information to help him be a better coach.

In order for this feedback to flow and be successful, one has to be trust-willing while relying on someone who is trustworthy. It demands that there be an openness on the recipient's part and that the person giving the feedback is someone who is reliable and dependable.

Who is your person or persons? How receptive and trust-*willing* are you to consider feedback? How can you ask more directly for what you want regarding feedback so it is particularly useful?

112

GET IT RIGHT OR BE RIGHT?

BRENÉ BROWN, THE PROLIFIC AUTHOR, SPEAKER, AND PODCASTER, has a quote I've used many times when helping clients navigate some of the relational challenges they encounter in the athletic arena, the workplace, or their personal life: "Are you looking to *be* right or get it right?"

Further to this point, Brown asks a challenging question in *Dare to Lead*: "When things get tough, do we lean into vulnerability and get curious, or do we self-protect in ways that move us away from our values?" In other words, do you acknowledge that you might not know it all or you might even be wrong, or do you shut down or disengage from the process of discovering the most valuable of objective truths?

I have witnessed virtually hundreds of conversations and meetings wherein finding "the truth" is apparently less of a consideration than promoting a given perspective as "right and true." All too often, our tendency is to argue or protect our perspective or our opinion at the expense of open-mindedness and curiosity about the viewpoints of others.

In my experience, many of **the best leaders and coaches are curious, have a lower need to be right all the time, are constantly**

questioning even their own assumptions, and are relentlessly asking for feedback. They use pertinent and thoughtful questions to get everyone in the system involved and contributing.

Similarly, the best teams I've been associated with have won titles and championships not because of a top-down sentiment that "I'm the boss (or the veteran or the most decorated), so shut up and do what I say," but as a result of cultivating an environment of collaboration, mutual respect, and a deep intention that is focused on identifying the truth and the best answers—independent of who discovers them and their status on the team.

Check your need to be right and strive to contribute as someone who is seeking the truth rather than seeking to be right or validated.

113

REACH THE CEILING OR **RAISE THE FLOOR?**

OFTENTIMES PEOPLE SEE THE BENEFITS OF MENTAL, PHYSICAL, technical, or tactical training as giving them a chance to reach their potential and to manifest peak experiences. Examples abound:

> "I want to be No. 1 in the world."
> "I want to win a championship ring."
> "I want to win a gold medal."
> "I want to be voted MVP."

These ultimate, top-of-your-game moments are fine to aspire to and can be a guiding light for those athletes willing to work hard enough to create a legitimate chance to earn them. Coaches and athletes frequently talk about what an athlete's "ceiling" is and how they can raise it—meaning, how they can realize their definitive potential.

I like to introduce athletes and teams to the perspective of working hard to *raise their floor*. **This speaks to an athlete or team's effort to be disciplined and consistent enough that even on those days when they are not at their best, they can remain reasonably competitive or successful.** Athletes speak of this in language like, "I'm doing pretty well despite just having my 'B' game," or "I'm making the most of an 'off' day."

The concept of raising the floor is a relatively simple one to understand, but the challenge is in the activities that align with giving oneself the best chance for this to happen.

Every athlete has their own unique challenges to overcome in order to minimize the negative impact of an "off day." This book details many suggestions for doing just that. Here are a few examples:

- Be intentional about keeping a healthy perspective.
- Direct self-talk to focus on what you *are* doing well versus spending too much energy on what's *not* going well.
- Bring your attention to the immediate task at hand and be committed to executing that task despite how things have been going.

Have as a goal not only the notion of improving your skills so you can continue to grow and move up the ladder in your craft, but also reinforce and appreciate the benefits of improving your average or raising your "floor" as well.

114

GO BE YOU

ATHLETES REGULARLY INTERPRET WHAT THEY BELIEVE THE demands of a situation to be. Whether or not those demands are factually accurate is irrelevant unless they do the work to think more objectively about the demands. What they believe the demands to be will guide them to act accordingly. In my experience, most athletes come up short of being objective about "the ask" in every training or competitive situation.

In high-stakes situations or against opponents who are perceived to be highly skilled, athletes often believe they need to do something special, work a little harder, or be a little more.

This typically leads to the "try too hard" mentality, and athletes can spiral out of their normal rhythm because they muscle up to be more intense or do something extra. This is exemplified in a phrase that I dislike, "This situation requires giving it 110 percent." No, I believe 100 percent will do just fine, thank you!

In these situations, I remind my clients that their job is to go be themselves. "Go be you" is something I text as a reminder to athletes at every level. Most athletes are aware of their abilities, their training reps, and their competitive successes. It is important that they use that awareness as information that they are pretty good at what they do.

No one can be more than who they are, but everyone has an opportunity to be themselves to the best of their ability without putting pressure on themselves to be bigger in any moment.

Learn to live with "Go be you" as an acceptable internal strategy. Work to increase self-awareness when you think about situations in such a way that it feels like doing more is necessary.

Working toward deep acceptance requires learning that "All I can do is be me, and it will be good enough or it won't. I can't be more special than I am, so I will be ready for however this turns out."

115

CONTROL THE SECOND THOUGHT

VIRTUALLY EVERY CLIENT WITH WHOM I'VE CONSULTED AT some point tells me they have thoughts that pop into their minds that are unhelpful or negative or just "crazy" (their word, not mine).

It comes as an immense relief for them to know that these initial "pop-in" thoughts are very rarely in anyone's control. On a daily basis, nearly every human has several things that happen that they didn't anticipate or desire.

The good news about this is that once people normalize this phenomenon, they can start working to diligently choose and control their second and subsequent thoughts and initial actions. It is powerful when you begin putting deliberate attention on responding to first thoughts with whatever it takes in the second and succeeding thoughts, such that the "power" of the first thought is minimized or eliminated.

The examples of this in sport could fill volumes. Here are some effective second-thought responses.

A golfer just prior to hitting a shot:

First thought: "Don't hit this drive out of bounds."

Second thought: "Of course I don't want to hit this out of bounds, so I'll pick a clear target of where I'd like it to go and commit through the impact zone."

A baseball player stepping into the batter's box:

First thought: "I never play well against this guy. He's struck me out a lot."

Second thought: "That may be historically true, but every at bat is a new opportunity. Let me pick up the spin on the ball early so it gives me the best chance to get a solid piece of the ball."

A triathlete on their walk to the starting line of a race:

First thought: "I have no chance today—look how fit all these people are."

Second thought: "I have trained hard and prepared well; I, too, am fit. I will focus on myself and keep my eyes off of how other people look. Comparisons are a killer to confidence."

Recognize your first thoughts, listen to these thoughts, give them power only if they serve you well and are factually accurate, and work to develop a consistent habit of responding wisely with second thoughts which minimize any damage the first thought might have done.

Essentially, this practice asks that you listen to yourself less and talk to yourself more!

116

MINIMIZE THE TIME YOU SPEND LOOKING IN THE GRASS

ROBERT SAPOLSKY WROTE A FASCINATING BOOK ENTITLED *Why Zebras Don't Get Ulcers: A Guide to Stress, Stress-Related Diseases, and Coping*. I have recommended it to dozens of my clients and gifted it to many others.

One of Sapolsky's essential premises is that zebras, unlike people, aren't constantly and with hypervigilance looking for danger. They go about their day with an inbred awareness that threat does exist in the form of predators such as lions. However, it is highly unlikely that zebras are stressing out about whether a lion is going to show up, when it will show up, how to manage oneself and protect the rest of the herd if one were to show up, etc. Zebras are simply living in the present moment, doing what they do. When danger or threat actually shows up, they react and respond with the attendant and necessary fight-or-flight response. Zebras do not constantly look into the grass and the weeds in anticipation of pending disaster.

In stark contrast, many people are regularly creating scenarios in their minds in the present moment that unnecessarily and unhealthily trigger physiological stress responses. Metaphorically, this equates to "looking in the grass," and every time something might look or sound like a threat, an internal chain reaction is triggered, which has the potential to create ulcers and a number of other medical and physical issues.

Glancing in the grass from time to time is probably a wise and beneficial thing for both humans and zebras to do. However, recognize your tendencies relative to how often you're "looking in there." What sorts of things set you into vigilance mode? How are you interpreting all of those moments when the "wind blows and the grass rustles a bit"? **There is a high payoff in learning to stay in the moment, calmly recognizing that regular hypervigilance is unnecessary.** Further to this point, identify and adjust the patterns of thought that contribute to the irrational notion that there is immediate danger "out there":

- Athletes overreacting to a coach's body language
- Teammates misinterpreting what someone intended in a brief conversation
- Officemates having hypothetical conversations in their own heads about some sort of negative outcome, only to become stressed over those made-up scenes

These are among the many types of situations in which we want to become more self-aware and better prepare ourselves to moderate our responses.

117

BRAIN BUDGETING

IT STANDS TO REASON THAT WE WOULD LIKE TO MINIMIZE THE cost or usage of our brain while maximizing what we use our brain to do. This is similar to how you manage your finances—you are not wanting to waste money unnecessarily or spend a lot of money on something that actually isn't that valuable.

I ask my clients to take me through a day or two of "normal" activities, and we scrutinize the cost/benefit ratio of what they are routinely undertaking to **identify opportunities where they can conserve brain energy and then expend it more intentionally in those times when a bit more brain energy might be helpful.** How much time and energy do we spend in frustration and anger in traffic? How much of our internal power do we expend worrying about a conversation we are avoiding or a task that stays in our "inbox" but we still ruminate about?

For example, say a golfer hits the ball off the tee into the woods. They then make a challenging shot to get it out onto the fairway—maybe hit a 9-iron to 25 feet and then make a 25-foot putt for par. Compare and contrast this hypothetical situation with a different attempt on that same hole which starts with a well-struck tee shot, an approach shot to 30 feet, and a 2-putt par from that distance. Which of those two scenarios will likely burn the most brain energy? Clearly, it's the first one. From worrying while walking to find the tee shot to navigating a difficult second shot to being excited about making a long putt, this first hole will demand more brain energy.

What I want the athlete to appreciate is that in either instance, we want to minimize excessive use of the brain during and after the hole as much as possible. Think of it as a metaphorical "dimmer switch" you can use to disengage from your situation—often through intentional distraction or mindfulness techniques. This way, you can mitigate the "brain burn" on the hole with the less-than-straightforward navigation.

As well, in any situation, it is important to recognize how much brain energy is burned by excessive emotion, overworrying, overanalyzing, etc. Where do you burn excessive brain fuel? How can you improve your brain budget in such a way that you preserve your "brain capital" for the moments that really require it?

Intentionally conserving our energy can be critical to having it available for optimal performance.

118

BE THE BEST ATHLETE **FOR THE TEAM**

BO HANSEN, CO-FOUNDER OF THE SPORT PROFILING COMPANY Athlete Assessments, has coined a wonderful phrase which deeply aligns with one of the philosophies that I promote. He encourages the athletes with whom he consults to **strive to be the best athlete for the team, not just the best athlete on the team.** This notion beautifully captures the essence of being a "team player" in sport. Finding ways to positively influence and affect the growth, development, and performance of others on one's team while also looking to make personal gains and improvements is selflessness personified.

There have been many great athletes in every sport on earth over many, many years. The ones who performed at the highest levels while also being attentive to their teammates' needs and successes are the ones who are the rarest, the most successful, and the most revered. Some can become *servant leaders* and take on actions that tangibly take care of their team members. Others are more *commanding leaders* who help others stay accountable, switched on, and giving of their maximum effort, which benefits everyone who is a part of the team. Still others are more like *cheerleaders*, constantly looking for ways to catch their teammates doing things well and encouraging and uplifting their peers independent of the situation.

What is also interesting about being the best athlete for the team is that it can be true for athletes who are not necessarily the most skilled or accomplished. There are innumerable examples of role players, benchwarmers, and substitutes who impacted their team's culture and made significant contributions to their team's successes without having much of a tangible impact in competitions.

Whatever your role on your team, in your company, or in your relationships, you have an opportunity to be purposeful about impacting the system around you. Clarify that intention and look to be someone who strives to influence and impact the growth, development, success, and enjoyment of the people around you.

While it may be a worthy endeavor to try to be the best you can be, wouldn't it be even more satisfying to assist others in that same endeavor along the way?

119

INTENT IS NOT THE SAME AS IMPERATIVE

THE BENEFIT AND VALUE OF HAVING CLEAR INTENTIONS ABOUT what you want is a theme that runs throughout *One Day Better.*

From a big-picture perspective, knowing what you'd like to accomplish in the long term, or having some sense of where you might like to "land," can guide you through challenging or confusing or difficult days. From a micro perspective, having well-defined intentions can be extremely useful in a moment—knowing where you'd like to hit this ball, knowing where you'd like that serve to end up, knowing what you'd like this routine to feel like, etc.

However, in setting these intentions, **don't make an intention into an imperative.** Having thought about or stated an intention or desire, some people have a tendency to make this intention or desire an absolute or a "have-to" in their minds.

As an example, in soccer or basketball or football, players will access a scouting report about their opponent that directs them toward a specific game plan, strategy, or tactic. These reports are often incredibly valuable in guiding a team to be successful. However, there are times when the opponent doesn't exactly do what was in the "scout," or conditions (weather, etc.) change the circumstances in a game. Players will sometimes take the scout as an imperative and act upon it so literally that they will have a hard time adapting if it's not 100 percent accurate. The "intent" of a game plan might sometimes be interpreted by athletes as an "imperative" that they must execute no matter what. This rigidity makes it difficult to "read the game" and adjust accordingly.

The people who see the intended execution as a guide and don't put the "have-to" spin on it are more successful. For them, this concept distinction is very clear. They find it helpful to accept that intention as a guide and learn to be at peace with some variation of it.

Make sure that you use your intentions as a clear guidepost but avoid putting pressure on yourself when attempting to execute on them. Work on tolerance for execution that is realistically acceptable, but not perfect.

120

SHARE YOUR MISTAKES

MATTHEW SYED'S BOOK *BLACK BOX THINKING* IS A VALUABLE read and holds insights that I've used hundreds of times in my consulting work. Among the more helpful notions for me and my clients is the idea that failure is necessary in order to grow. Learning from failures results in lessons that can guide you toward mastery.

Here's the idea: It is valuable for a culture or a system—or a team—to share stories about what happened when they made mistakes. By sharing these stories, they hope to decrease the likelihood that someone within the system (family, team, staff, etc.) will have to suffer failure to learn the same lesson. The "black box" in the title of Syed's book refers to the recording device in airplanes that the airline industry has used to make enormous strides in minimizing air disasters over many years. **Information gathered is routinely shared with others in the industry, including any and all things that contributed to mistakes made, in the hope of preventing others from making the same mistake.**

In the context of team sports, what would it be like if each athlete had the humility to openly admit to their failings or mistakes so that the athletes next to them could learn the same lessons and shorten the learning curve? Not everyone would have to "learn it the hard way." As well, everyone would be intentionally contributing to the growth of every teammate, which would be a productive way to help a team realize its ultimate potential.

I facilitate this with many of the sports programs I work with every year when the freshman or rookies arrive. I invite the returning athletes to speak about the lessons they learned through mistakes made in their first year on the team. The feedback I consistently receive is that this session is invaluable to incoming athletes in navigating a new environment, and for returning athletes it showcases humility and a willingness to guide their new teammates toward success.

It is often embarrassing and sometimes even humiliating to tell people of our failures, deficits, or blunders. However, in order to contribute to whatever system you find yourself in, consider the value to the "greater good of all" if you share what you've learned from these moments. I would hope for your sake, and the sake of those in your immediate sphere, you'd be willing to have the humility to enhance the knowledge of those around you.

121

IMPOSTOR SYNDROME

ATHLETES ARE NOT IMMUNE TO THE DIFFICULTIES PRESENTED by impostor syndrome, or feeling as though their accomplishments or successes are invalid, not good enough, or not attributable to their own skill or work. Impostor syndrome presents itself in a variety of ways, most notably when someone says something like:

"I don't feel like I deserve this."
"I just feel lucky to be here."
"I don't feel like I belong at this level."
"I am not good enough to compete in this league."

While certainly it may be true at times that luck comes into play or an athlete is not yet skilled enough to be competitive as they advance up the levels of expertise, impostor syndrome is distinctive because the person feels this way despite clear evidence to the contrary. When there is plenty of data to gather that could objectively spell out why the accomplishments are valid and how the person earned such status or recognition, their competence is greater than their confidence.

In 1985 Joan C. Harvey and Cynthia Katz published a book about impostor phenomena entitled *If I'm So Successful, Why Do I*

Feel Like a Fake? This book was massively influential in my career, as it helped guide me toward assisting those who thought they were a fraud or were obsessively worried about being "exposed" or found to be unworthy.

This is difficult work for anyone to undertake who is challenged by this pattern of thinking. Here's the best advice I can offer in this short exposure to the concept: **If you suffer from impostor syndrome, I encourage you to do as objective an accounting as possible of the substantiating evidence that likely exists to provide credibility to your successes.** Often people stuck in this loop will invalidate or minimize their accomplishments with statements like:

> "Why would I pat myself on the back for that? I was just doing my job."
> "Anyone in that situation would have done the same thing."
> "That's not that big of a deal."

Essentially, they are disqualifying the positives.

Doing the personal discovery and improvement work to "own" your success is not easy, but I strongly encourage familiarity with this affliction so you know how to get into a healthier space with your thoughts around your abilities and your achievements.

122

RESPECT THE GAME

ANSON DORRANCE RETIRED IN 2024 AS THE UNIVERSITY OF North Carolina's women's soccer team head coach, where he guided the Tar Heels to the NCAA finals 24 times, winning 21 national championships. One of the quotes he purportedly had up in the locker room there is this: "Respect your opponent enough to annihilate them."

I've used this quote over the years with athletes and teams who have a tendency to take their foot off the gas or decrease their effort when they are winning with ease or competing against an opponent they perceive to be less competent.

The goal behind the lesson is to help athletes appreciate that whatever game you play, you demonstrate respect by giving it 100 percent effort at all times. Backing down from your best effort feels, to me, disrespectful of the intent of competition. I have worked with athletes and teams who have been on the receiving end of this dynamic. If their opponent backs off or lets up in competition, it comes across as charity, patronizing, or even condescending—it feels like an insult.

I would say that in the majority of cases, the athlete or team "backing off" has good intentions. They don't want to run up the score or make the other team look worse. They don't want to embarrass the other athletes. Unfortunately, though, backing off often has the opposite effect.

In some situations, making adjustments from a tactical perspective is warranted, but I do not believe it is warranted from a physical effort perspective. For example, putting in substitutes and/or adjusting the aggressiveness of playing strategy seems respectful. Reducing effort, clowning around, or laughing while playing down to the perceived level of the opponent seems very disrespectful.

Bottom line: **Do what the game demands and the sport deserves.** Maximize effort in spite of the scoreboard or skill set of all involved. This type of play constitutes the highest reverence for the game.

123

ANSWER YOUR **RHETORICAL QUESTIONS**

GENERALLY, A RHETORICAL QUESTION IS PUT OUT THERE AS A statement rather than an actual question, but athletes regularly find themselves in the nonproductive habit, particularly when they are under stress, of asking these questions and then letting them just hang.

What is wrong with me today?
Why can't I get it right?
Why does this always happen to me?
How did I do something so stupid?
What the heck is going on right now?

The list is virtually endless. These are the types of things shouted out in between points by tennis and volleyball and racquetball players. They come to mind in between shots by golfers; in between pitches or plays in baseball, softball, and football; and in ongoing play in basketball, hockey, and soccer. Track-and-field athletes, swimmers, gymnasts, rodeo participants—no matter who the athlete is, these questions are pervasive in virtually every sport, whether they are spoken internally or out loud.

Athletes tell me that if they leave the question unanswered, it increases stress, generates no solutions or alternatives, and leads to either a decrease in confidence or a sense of being out of control in the moment. This is why I propose they actually answer the question in the interest of productively impacting the emotions they are experiencing.

> ***"What is wrong with me today?"***
> "Nothing is wrong with me—I'm just not yet performing like I usually do. Let's get back to refocusing on the next rep."
>
> ***"Why can't I get it right?"***
> "I can get it right—I'm just having a difficult time right now. Slow yourself down in between points and make an intentional adjustment."
>
> ***"Why does this always happen to me?"***
> "It doesn't always happen to you. It happens to you sometimes, but often it does not. Don't have a pity party. Stop feeling sorry for yourself. You've had your share of bad luck today, but things can certainly turn around."
>
> ***"How did I do something so stupid?"***
> "You did that because you were rushing and didn't read the defense as well as you're capable of doing. Get back to doing what you do well."
>
> ***"What the heck is going on right now?"***
> "You had a lead and now you're behind. Now let's go forward. Get clear on how you're going to adapt to what your opponent is doing."

The resolution involves answering the question factually and objectively, reminding yourself of your ability to adjust and execute something well, and then often adding a redirect to the next play, the next moment, or the next point.

When you build a habit of answering your rhetorical questions rationally and intelligently, you develop a skill that can help you overcome a lot of challenging moments in your sport.

124

HOW WOULD YOU ACT IF THE OUTCOME **WAS CERTAIN?**

SOMETIMES I CREATE HYPOTHETICAL SITUATIONS FOR MY ATHLETES in order to tease out some subtlety in their thinking or overall mindset for us to discuss. One of my favorite questions to pose is, "How would you feel and act if you were certain or guaranteed that everything was going to turn out just like you were hoping?"

Invariably, nearly everyone talks about how much more relaxed they'd be, how much calmer and more comfortable. There is almost always a thread about how much more they'd enjoy the experience and how much more present they'd allow themselves to be versus being preoccupied with worry or concern over the future.

Then I ask them my next question: "What sort of impact might that kind of internal environment have on the quality of your training and/or competitive performance?" In virtually every instance, the client acknowledges they would likely perform better.

It's interesting what happens from this point. Sometimes, certainly not always, the client makes the direct connection between their stress over future uncertainty and their thought choices in the present situation. They have increased awareness of how they are likely contributing to their training or performance challenges because, at some level, they are worried about how things are going to work out.

Sometimes it is as simple as allowing for moments to consider the real possibility of success—not as an expectation, but as a viable option. There are times I have experienced alongside clients where a daily practice of taking a moment to consider the possibility of achieving the goal(s) suppresses their stress and internal distractedness in a marginal but meaningful way. That slight adjustment made on a daily basis can compound over time and have a tremendously constructive impact.

Allow yourself some instances of thinking and acting "as if" some version of success were inevitable.

125

HAUNTED BY THE GHOST OF THE PAST

EASILY, ONE OF THE MOST CHALLENGING SITUATIONS AN ATHLETE can face is dealing with an injury. Disappointment, frustration, fear, anxiety, doubts, and much more can feel overwhelming as they go through the diagnosis, intervention, and/or rehabilitation process.

From a psychological perspective, it's helpful to work very intentionally to apply the One Day Better method to the effort to return to practice and play. Many athletes, even once they are fully rehabilitated, find themselves putting too much attention on how they were playing before they were injured:

"I was so much stronger then."
"I could jump so much higher before my injury."
"I was playing so well in the days leading up to when I got hurt."

All of these truths could be used as a way to build belief in one's abilities and skill potential. However, most of the time these sorts of statements are used as a way to put an emphasis on what the athlete is *not able to do* right now. The gap between where you are and where you were can be a big distraction. In essence, you are haunted by the ghost of your past (with a tip of the cap to *A Christmas Carol*).

When your mind wanders to where you were, how you were, or what you were pre-injury, work diligently to redirect your focus to what is true about your strengths and opportunities today. How can you improve on what you did yesterday? How can you move in the direction of progress so you can acknowledge or affirm today's win?

Accepting the reality of the temporary regression in strength or applicable skill or fitness level, and then comparing yourself to your yesterday, is going to be much more productive and emotionally healthy than looking in your rearview mirror at how you were doing before you got injured. This same notion applies to athletes as they grow older and their physical skills naturally diminish. Those athletes who are successful in playing well past their "prime" generally have a high level of acceptance of what they *can* do with their body currently, instead of lamenting what their body no longer allows them to do.

126

PROGRESS IS MESSY

ATHLETES AND THEIR COACHES AT TIMES CAN BECOME IMPATIENT with the process of skill development or frustrated with the slow speed at which some accomplishments take place.

In particular, I frequently hear athletes lament the fact that their progress is going slowly, or it feels like they're going backward, or they just generally feel unsatisfied with the way things have been going lately. Coaches will sometimes express disbelief at "how long it's taking them to 'get it'" when athletes struggle to integrate some new mechanical or tactical element.

When this happens, it is beneficial to engage in a deeper exploration of what is going on. Progress toward anything worthwhile is messy—growth does not go in a straight line "up and to the right." There are *a lot* of days when you fall flat, make mistakes, and even regress. Coinciding with these are the days that feel like massive growth or a steady trend in a productive direction, and a lot of days that feel static or like a plateau.

The point is to help normalize the fact that no one in the history of success in any domain has had a straightforward path to their metaphorical mountaintop. Instead, **see those days that feel like a pause or a backslide for what they are—a typical day in the life of an**

achiever. Be mindful not to make one day out to be something more than it might actually be: *Oh no, I'm never going to make it like this! Or, I'm working so hard and making no progress.*

Certainly, scrutinizing and doing an ongoing assessment of the effectiveness of your development can be helpful and is occasionally recommended and warranted. Let's just not have the doubts and worries and judgments about the daily struggles override what is likely to be objectively true—if you're doing the work and putting in the reps toward the success you desire, it could be that you're just not seeing it yet. Be intentional about accurately interpreting what's going on today. Today is another point plotted on your growth chart, which is oriented along a *long-term trend* of up and to the right.

The time frame between "not getting it" and "getting it" can be days, weeks, months, or even years. We do not know how long it's going to take to "get it." What we *do* know is that the time in the interim is where growth and discovery occur, and this is a necessary and non-negotiable juncture in the process of achieving excellence.

127

GOOD, BETTER, HOW

AMONG THE SIMPLE SUGGESTIONS I MAKE TO ATHLETES, TEAMS, and coaches is to keep a journal or logbook or diary. Within that go-to place to store all things related to their sport (or life), I recommend they embark on a simple but effective exercise.

As a part of their daily journaling experience, which is personal and unique to all, I propose that there is structure to at least one part of the daily process. At the end of the day, I suggest that my client spend time reflecting on these prompts:

Good: What you did well today.
"I really was hitting the ball better today when I was focusing on my tempo rather than my technique."

Better: What you didn't do as well as you would like and would like to improve upon.
"I had a hard time keeping my attention on my tempo when I was hitting my driver on the range because I kept stressing about my mechanics."

How: Steps you will take as soon as possible to make those improvements.
"Tomorrow I am going to be very intentional that my success criteria with my driver be about having clear focus on my rhythm and tempo. How I contact the ball or where the ball goes is going to be a secondary consideration for now."

In building a daily habit of "good/better/how" thinking, I get feedback consistently that my clients believe it helps them **learn more fully, find solutions more rapidly, and stay more focused and intentional about the mechanisms and actions that lead to improvement.**

Be like many great athletes and take the time to do this short exercise to give yourself daily feedback and set yourself up for tomorrow's successes!

128

COMMIT TO GETTING CLEAN DATA

THE DISTINCTION BETWEEN TRUST AND COMMITMENT FACTORS into the working relationship of an athlete and a coach.

One of the elements of this is the notion that independent of trust, one has the option to be fully committed to something or not. One of the reasons why this is of such value is that in order to gather "clean data" on whether something works or not, we want to be able to see if the change we are committing to has the intended impact. This necessitates a "pure experiment" of employing the committed actions so that the feedback gathered is accurate.

When a coach prescribes a change in an athlete's training regimen, it is common for the athlete to have some small doubt or distrust in the change, even if they have faith in their coach. I'm regularly advising athletes to go "all in" on the change, even if they don't yet trust it, because it's the only way for them to see if it actually works or not. Frequently, athletes will covertly make micro changes to the workouts in order for them to feel more comfortable, secure, or in control. This effectively "contaminates" the experiment because we can no longer know if what the coach prescribed would have worked.

When a coach suggests a change in tactics or technique or anything else, I ask athletes to give it enough of a committed trial to

gather the objective feedback required. If the change you've executed works well, then that committed process increases your trust factor. If, on the other hand, a committed trial does not work as well as hoped, it gives you valid feedback and the information necessary to go back to your coach to have a conversation about the change.

129

ARE YOU THE HUNTER OR THE HUNTED?

THIS IS AMONG THE MANY INTERESTING PSYCHOLOGICAL phenomena in sport, and it reveals valuable information about the interior environment of the athlete.

When athletes see themselves as *the hunter*, they are in their training session or in their competition with a mentality of going for it and the sense that there is nothing to lose. In these situations, athletes and teams generally play more freely and with more productive aggression and abandon, regardless of the circumstances:

> "We're this far behind—we might as well go for it."
> "We have very little chance, but let's give it all we've got to see if we can catch up."

On the other hand, a perception of being *the hunted* can trigger a sense of being chased or a worry about getting caught, which can lead athletes to play it safe or protect their lead or throttle back:

> "Let's not lose our lead."
> "They're not that far behind us."

"Let's make sure we're mistake-free so we don't let them back into the contest."

Further complicating things, an athlete's perception can flip-flop back and forth in a very short period of time within a singular contest. The ebb and flow in a number of sports allows for athletes to think multiple times within a contest things like, "I've got this" or "I have no chance."

Recognize that no matter how you see yourself, it is just a perception. While it may be true that you are in the lead or trailing on the scoreboard, future-tripping about how it may end up only feeds into more "hunter" or "hunted" types of thoughts. These then lead to playing freely and aggressively or playing tentatively and "not to lose."

Firstly, recognize when you are doing this before or during a contest. Secondly, **work diligently and intentionally to change your perspective on this in real time with an emphasis on a "going for it" and "nothing to lose" mentality.** This is actionably displayed by being aggressive and assertive and committed, independent of where you are on the scoreboard. Athletes and teams who are the most disciplined in their approach to situations and act with controlled aggression independent of the circumstances are the ones most likely to have consistent success.

Practice and play like you are the hunter—if your sights are set on excellence and mastery, you will *always* be a hunter!

130

GET CLARITY AROUND **PERSONAL SUCCESS CRITERIA**

THE WORLD SURROUNDING ATHLETES AND THEIR TEAMS IS constantly reminding them of how they *should* measure their successes. Winning, prize money, rankings, fame, scholarships, and endorsements are among the hallmarks of success.

While there is nothing wrong with people aspiring to these things, it is exceedingly beneficial for athletes to generate their own personal success criteria. Furthermore, athletes benefit from having clarity on their short-term success criteria during virtually every competition and training session.

As an athlete, of course you want to win and get all the stuff that comes along with that, but in today's game/match/contest/tournament, what are your success criteria that will give you a good chance to win or accomplish those desired outcomes?

Helping athletes define their daily success criteria is something I do quite often. **Start by asking yourself, *What does a "win" look like today?***

- Will you be integrating a new technique into your competition to see how it feels and figure out if it works?

- Are you focused on improving your body language after a disappointment in the contest?
- Do you intend to minimize negative self-talk when self-doubt or wavering belief start to creep into your mind?

The list of examples of success criteria is virtually infinite. There are so many small but valuable things that can be honed or emphasized or given specific attention in order to build habits or generate data or information that the options can be mind-boggling. A vast number of athletes do not take the time to identify a success criterion (or two) within their control. Consequently, they are likely to get so wrapped up in winning or losing that they forget to pay attention to the things that give them the greatest chance to win.

Build a daily habit around getting clarity on the success criteria that you control, and then give yourself objective and honest feedback at the end of each day. This simple practice can result in tremendous growth and mental discipline that can be leveraged into actions that increase the likelihood of positive outcomes and subsequent consequences.

131

GET DISTANCE FROM YOURSELF

IN ETHAN KROSS'S GROUNDBREAKING BOOK *CHATTER*, HE does a deep dive into our internal dialogue or self-talk, describing how our self-talk starts, evolves, and is sustained.

One of the findings among the research shared in the book is that the more one immerses oneself in their self-talk, the more vivid and real and impactful it can be. Thus, when things are going well, thinking about it, reflecting on it, acknowledging it, and "banking it" can be very productive.

On the other hand, it is also true that deep immersion in negative experiences has the effect of making them more impactful.

Kross recommends an array of adjustments that can be made, two of which are "distancing strategies" I have repeatedly used with my clients:

1. Speak to yourself intentionally in second or third person rather than first person.
2. Ask yourself future-oriented questions about how important this moment is going to be for you down the road.

In the first instance, many of my clients have found it helpful to speak to themselves in second or third person when they are angry, frustrated, or losing emotional control or stability.

> "C'mon, Jeff, you're better than that. Keep your focus sharp," as opposed to "I always lose my focus! What's wrong with me right now?"
> "You're not moving your feet like you're capable of right now," versus "I am so slow, and I'm not getting to the ball well."

The feedback I have received from clients who have tried this simple technique has sold me on the efficacy of this method.

As for the future-oriented adjustment, it would look something like this:

> "You're angry right now, and justifiably. That was really unfortunate. Now, truthfully, how will what just happened impact your life 10 years from now?"
> "Yes, that was an untimely error, but if you keep fighting that won't matter at the end of the game."

We are trying to influence the athlete's perspective of the importance and effect of whatever they are currently emotional about.

With either or both of these methods, **you can make an immediate and long-term impact on the quality of your internal environment and increase the chances that your self-talk will influence you in a constructive manner.**

132

WHAT IS UNDER THE TREE?

ONE OF THE MYRIAD CHALLENGES TO THE PSYCHE OF AN ATHLETE is *anticipatory anxiety*. For a great number of athletes, the lead-up to their competitions creates as much—and often times more—anxiety than the actual execution at the competition itself.

I encourage athletes who feel this way to see upcoming competitions in a more constructive light. I ask them to anticipate their events in the same way they may have anticipated Christmas morning as a child. Many people can recall the countdown to Christmas Day. The anticipation of what Santa might bring or what might be under the tree generated excitement and eagerness.

In the same way, as an adult, we can better tap into the joy of future competitive moments if we reduce expectations around *what we are going to get* and instead approach the event from a place of excitement and curiosity: *What will the gift be?* **It's a much more exciting and healthy internal space that reduces anxiety around outcomes.** It also keeps us from overthinking—*what if I don't get what I want?*

If we anticipate certain gifts and they don't happen to be in the box when all is said and done, of course that's disappointing. Contrarily, if we do "get what we want," that's exciting! In competitions, we don't have control over what's in the box. But what we *can* do is have a mindset going into these events that promotes inquisitiveness, excitement, and appreciation for the opportunity to experience whatever the day brings.

133

SWING THE CLUB VS. HIT THE SHOT

I HAVE LEARNED SO MUCH FROM SO MANY GREAT ATHLETES over the years. Many of my conversations with athletes have instigated my own inquiries into the intricacies of how people think.

In nearly every sport, there are a number of athletes who have a difficult time bringing their practice "stuff" to the competitive arena. I hear all the time about how "I was practicing so well yesterday, and I was terrible today," or "I was hitting it so well on the range, but when I went on the course, it wasn't the same." This idea applies generally in every sport. I also hear it from executives who felt good about "nailing" their presentation when they were practicing it, and then "when it counted," they didn't execute it as well. The reasons for detrimental influences are as innumerable and distinct as the people who suffer through them. I will share one possible contributing dynamic here.

Many years ago, I was talking with a PGA Tour player who had a tendency to have his attention in completely different places on the range when practicing or warming up versus in competition on the golf course. We discovered that he had his attention on *swinging the club* on the range, but on the golf course his attention was on *hitting a certain type of shot*. It was extremely helpful for him to recognize that difference, and we talked through the three simple options for making an adjustment: 1) keep things the way they were—which wasn't working very well; 2) adjust his range attention to match his course attention; 3) adjust his course attention to match his range attention.

What we found in the exploration, and what I have shared with hundreds of clients in the years since, is that there is no singular "right way" to do this. **Either club-related attention or shot-related attention may work for a particular player, but once they are aware of this concept, they can be more intentional with finding congruence and consistency.**

This notion works in virtually every sport. When you are practicing your skill, where is your attention directed? In a defensive drill in soccer, you may be very focused on your footwork, which works nicely, but then in the game you might instead get overly fixated on the ball. In tennis you might be very successful in your serving practice, feeling the snap of your racket as it goes through the ball, but then you direct your attention in the match to the target, which may or may not be optimal.

Even more fascinating (to a sport development nerd like me!) is that there may be times in the skill acquisition process when the timing of when and where to "park" attention changes. An example would be a golfer who is making a swing change with their instructor. In the short term, while refining the swing toward becoming more automatic, it may benefit them to have their attention on "swing the club" and then it may (or may not) benefit them after they have integrated the improvement in their swing to shift back to attention on "hit the shot."

In many sports, this has translation into body awareness vs. target awareness or feel/internal awareness vs. visual/external awareness.

As with everything I discuss, the only thing that really matters here is to get more identification of the options available to you and to be more intentional about employing your preferred option very consistently.

134

COCKY OR CONFIDENT?

CONFIDENCE IS ONE OF THE CONSTRUCTS I SPEND A GREAT DEAL of my consulting time discussing with clients. A specific element of confidence that is often brought to my attention is the fine line between confidence and arrogance. There are a large number of athletes, properly humble, who deny themselves the confidence and self-belief they've earned because they are concerned about their belief or confidence being construed by others as arrogance or cockiness.

One of the ways I address this with my clients is to have them communicate objective truths in response to direct questions about their accomplishments or achievements. In other words, I propose that athletes simply state what is factually accurate:

"Yes, I won a gold medal at the last Olympics."
"Yes, I have been ranked No. 1 in the world."
"Yes, I won the club golf championship last year."
"Yes, I played Division 1 soccer in college."
"Yes, I was a starter on the team this year."

Frequently, people will downplay their accomplishments or discount their objective successes, starting their answers to questions with: "I don't want to brag . . . "

Certainly, there are those out there who many of us would agree lack humility and *are* cocky or arrogant. For me, a big distinction is whether they are telling people about their accomplishments without being asked or if they are responding to a direct inquiry. As former Duke basketball Coach Mike Krzyzewski once put it, "Arrogance requires advertising. Confidence speaks for itself."

Allowing yourself to acknowledge the work put in and accomplishments realized is foundational to the inner confidence of knowing who you are as a person and owning what you've done. Messaging to yourself about these things frequently is the hallmark of many great athletes. Many of the most accomplished athletes with whom I've worked have a "quiet love affair with themselves." I think the "quiet" part is what separates confidence from cockiness, with the exception of being loud and proud about it when asked!

135

USE YESTERDAY AS FUEL

IT REQUIRES A LOT OF PERSEVERANCE AND RESILIENCE TO repeatedly train and compete in any endeavor and deal with the natural ups and downs that occur. Great athletes view failure as information that guides them toward additional growth and development and success. This is another characteristic that each of us can assess within ourselves. What are you saying to yourself, and how do you feel after you face adversity?

The most successful among us cannot wait to get back out there tomorrow, even if we've been unsuccessful today. **This entails a choice to see today's challenges and setbacks as informative and inspiring.** Whereas "tough days at the office" cause many people to struggle with feeling discouraged or disgruntled, the best of us are motivated by those difficult days.

This is not to say that in those moments of frustration, disappointment, or failure, athletes aren't experiencing those raw emotions. However, I am saying that "the best" have developed an intentional habit of turning that into fuel for tomorrow's opportunities.

A high-profile professional tennis player with whom I worked was rising up the world rankings on her ultimate climb to being ranked No. 1 in the world. I distinctly remember that after a tough loss in a Grand Slam match, she said, "That really sucked. That match was painful and heartbreaking, but I now know what to work on in order to beat [that woman] next time." And she did.

How enthusiastic are you to go try it again tomorrow if things didn't go well today? Are you letting your interpretation of today cast a gloomy cloud over subsequent attempts, or do you bring eagerness and determination to the next day?

To understand your own tendencies and keep redirecting yourself to a motivated path can be the difference between achieving your dreams or falling short.

136

COME TO YOUR SENSES

ONE OF THE MOST USEFUL TOOLS THAT MY CLIENTS IMPLEMENT is being intentional about being in their senses. What this means, practically, is that rather than being in their head with their thoughts, they train themselves to minimize thoughts (and brain-wave activity!) by directing their attention to their senses.

One of the suggestions I make is that the athlete have a specific strategy to get in their senses when they find themselves overanalyzing or becoming internally distracted. Here are some examples:

- A tennis player might be deliberate in directing their eyes on their strings in between points (vision) while feeling their feet on the court (kinesthetic or body awareness).
- A golfer might be purposeful in counting their steps to their next shot (body awareness) while looking for birds or squirrels or flowers (vision).
- A baseball or softball player who is playing defense might listen for a unique sound in between pitches (auditory) and swipe their foot in the dirt or grass (body awareness) while taking a deep breath (body awareness).

- A distance runner might listen to the staccato rhythm of their feet (auditory) while simultaneously feeling their initial foot strike (body awareness).

These types of strategies have been exceedingly effective with many of my clients, as they have developed a go-to strategy either between every task (points, pitches, shots, etc.) or as a go-to when they feel their mind spiraling out of control. Being in their senses becomes a reset strategy and a redirection of their attention away from what they're thinking and toward what they're physically experiencing.

It's a simple, but highly impactful, grounding and centering skill to master as you continue to work toward self-regulation.

137

COMPLETE YOUR COMPASSION

I HAVE BEEN SO FORTUNATE IN MY CAREER TO HAVE BEEN intimately involved in deep, honest, and vulnerable discussions with some of the kindest and most character-driven people on earth.

I literally cannot count the number of clients I have had who cared deeply about others, who reached out into their community to help those in need, or who showed deep compassion for their fellow human beings. Interestingly, many of these same people struggle at times with sharing those same characteristics with themselves. A quote that I share with many of my clients speaks to this: "If your compassion does not extend to yourself, it is incomplete."

Being kind to oneself, showing grace and compassion, and minimizing self-judgment can make or break even those who have the greatest potential for success.

To my knowledge, there is no secret formula for being more compassionate with oneself. I encourage my clients to follow a few simple steps:

1. Recognize and admit that this is a challenge, if it indeed is true.
2. Examine the self-talk you use in difficult situations and contrast that with how you speak to others in similar circumstances.

3. Prioritize making consistent, small gains in changing this feedback.
4. Do the work to act upon this reprioritization in a disciplined fashion to "rewire" and build a habit of being kinder and more loving to yourself.
5. If you find it helpful, journal about or voice record these moments to "get them out of your head."

It is as simple and as difficult as that. Have a goal and clear intention to be more kind to *you*.

138

DON'T LET **PREPARATION** GO INTO OVERTIME

SOME COACHES "OVERCOACH" THEIR ATHLETES. THE REASONS behind this tendency are unique to the individual, and there are literally hundreds of variations on this theme. "Why" a coach does this can be worthwhile to explore. More important is for them to understand the ramifications of how this behavior impacts athletes and how it can negatively affect performance.

Without getting into the science behind skill acquisition, suffice it to say that most researchers agree that learning a new skill requires a number of repetitions before it can be executed "automatically," with minimal or no thinking about the "how" of it. These early stages of skill-building demand consistent vigilance to attain a certain level of proficiency.

Once the skill has been reasonably learned, however, most all relevant research regarding skill acquisition speaks to the necessity for the person to have autonomy to essentially "figure it out" in the final stages that precede expertise. This is where I see many coaches err and consequently, many athletes overthink.

My experience has been that if the coach has a strong grip on the joystick, attempting to overengineer or control their athlete's actions once they are at a certain level of proficiency, it can undermine the athlete's instinctive and organic ways of applying what they've learned. The athlete will be prone to work to "please the coach" or "do what the coach wants" as opposed to reading the situation, reacting, and/or using their own athleticism. Some athletes do this to themselves, which is the classic "paralysis by analysis" as they try to micromanage all they are doing within their athletic endeavor. This frequently short-circuits the natural flow of applying the skills they've worked hard to acquire.

To be clear, coaches giving this type of leash can in some instances mean that the athlete doesn't perform as well in those moments. I would argue that the long-term benefit of an athlete figuring out their own style of application that is most effective for them outweighs most short-term costs.

As a coach or manager of an athlete or team or staff, be aware of the cost/benefit of overinstructing once a certain level of competence has been obtained.

139

BUILD STRENGTH THROUGH ADVERSITY

IN STRENGTH AND CONDITIONING CIRCLES, THERE IS A NOTION around "shocking the system" in order to potentially stimulate physical growth. The logic is that subjecting the muscle to new stimulus or stress will cause it to grow bigger and stronger. Over time, the same stimulus will become less effective because the muscle adapts to the work, so an adjustment is needed in order for it to continue to grow.

I believe this is potentially true for our mindset too. Some of the greatest growth to a person's mindset and overall mentality is often stimulated by what they learn from facing adversity. Intentionally putting their athletes through intensive situational adversity is how some of the best coaches train their athletes to build coping skills to assist them in managing adversity in competitions.

Examples of this might be a tennis coach who intentionally calls line calls incorrectly to see how their player manages the "unfair" treatment. Basketball coaches might call fouls on one possession wherein a player barely makes contact and then, the next time down the court, they don't blow the whistle when greater contact has taken place. Baseball coaches might "squeeze or open" the strike zone and call balls and strikes inconsistently to stress either the batter or the pitcher—or both.

These manufactured situations are deliberate attempts to shock the system and get the athletes to build response sets that are productive. Nearly every training session and competition will provide opportunities, and clearly there are many moments outside of sport where the natural adversities in life are encountered. Some athletes will take it upon themselves to deliberately place themselves in adverse situations to see how to "find a way out."

Athletes who embrace these difficult moments as necessary for growth and are willing to shock their systems in order to see how they handle it generally figure out answers to difficult situations more rapidly. They develop a systematic way of internally coping with unforeseen events.

Work toward an appreciation for what adversity can teach you about your own mechanisms of resilience. Seeking out challenge and fostering hardship management can be invaluable to your overall growth and development.

Haruki Murakami describes how our challenges shape us in *Kafka on the Shore*: "And once the storm is over, you won't remember how you made it through, how you managed to survive. You won't even be sure whether the storm is really over. But one thing is certain. When you come out of the storm, you won't be the same person who walked in. That's what this storm's all about."

140

NAME THE MONSTER

WHEN ATHLETES OR COACHES COME TO ME WITH ANXIETY AND worry and fear about a negatively imagined future event, I often invite them to name the "monster" that is frightening them.

> "I have to play well this season in order for me to be drafted highly."
> "If my team doesn't win, I may lose my job."
> "If I don't play better, I might lose my starting position."
> "I might lose my sponsor if I don't get on the podium."

In their effort to support these athletes and coaches, some people will try to convince them that these fears are irrational or that they aren't true. I take a different approach, pushing into the reality that what they fear might actually happen. I then ask them to "go down the rabbit hole" and describe out loud the monster they're creating in their head. I actually want them to speak to what they fear might happen, and more importantly, how they will cope with it if it does in fact happen.

Some of them are resistant to talk about their fears:

> "If I think about what my life might be like if I don't get drafted, I might not work as hard."
> "I think if I allow myself to consider an alternative to success in that situation, I might increase the likelihood that I will not be successful."

Too many athletes and coaches internalize and try to stuff down their worries and doubts and fears. They don't see that this failure alternative or "monster" is not as scary as they make it out to be in their heads. Once they allow themselves to actually look at what their life might be like if they don't get the success they are desiring, they see that despite feeling disappointment, and likely some sadness, their alternatives are generally not as bad or scary as they are making them out to be. Rather than having this monster in their head be something they consciously or unconsciously avoid, they can make peace with their backup plan or alternative path. This in turn frequently frees up the athlete or coach to embrace their current opportunity with a less obstructed and less threatened internal environment. The realization that "I'm going to be OK either way" often brings relief and helps quiet the fear, which generates improved performance potential.

If you're scared of an outcome, name it and find a way to make peace with it. Recognize the strength within you to manage that situation even though you would not choose for it to happen. Then go work to slay the monster!

141

MOTIVATION WILL COME AND GO

THE CONCEPT OF MOTIVATION IS A HOT TOPIC IN ATHLETIC environs, prompting a host of questions:

- What is the source of an athlete's motivation, and how deep does it run?
- How can coaches and organizations create an environment that motivates athletes?
- How can an athlete obtain and/or sustain motivation?
- Are some motivators unhealthy and others healthier?

I direct athletes and teams toward the idea that there may be big-picture motivations, daily motivations, and obvious or subtle motivations. In any of these contexts, motivation will wax and wane over time. Some days, athletes are very aware of what stirs them and they feel invigorated and intentional about it. As well, there are other days where they just "aren't feeling it" or are challenged to find the "why" that stimulates them in a particular moment.

While you may not be feeling motivated in a given moment, you still have the option to be disciplined in your actions and behaviors.

Not "feeling it" but still having the discipline to complete a workout with good effort and good technique elicits the same ultimate outcomes as feeling motivated right from the outset to complete a hard workout—and then doing it. In the end, it's about doing the job whether you feel like it or not. This demands actionable discipline—not just in thought, but also in deed.

There are many circumstances where you are not feeling motivated, and in some of those instances there may be time and benefit in exploring how to increase motivation. Some situations, however, require a setting aside of the motivation exploration so you can get shit done *right now*. The time for motivation contemplation can come later.

If you are unmotivated in a moment when it's time to do work, be disciplined in your actions and override your tendency to procrastinate or pull the throttle back. You do this by producing your maximum methodical effort.

142

YOU ARE YOUR MOST IMPORTANT **OPPONENT**

HAVING CONSULTED ACROSS A MULTITUDE OF DIFFERENT SPORTS, I find the similarities and differences between and among the sports as it relates to the mental/emotional component fascinating. Individual sport athletes versus team sport athletes. Requisite closed skills such as hitting a golf ball, serving a tennis ball, or shooting a free throw versus open skills where the game is dynamic and ever-changing and an opponent may be attempting to defend you or throw off your game. In golf as an example, it is always a closed skill. No one is trying to block your shot or tackle you while you hit your putt. Soccer, on the other hand, is nearly always an open skill, as almost every moment is fluid and dynamic. In some sports like tennis or volleyball, there is the closed skill of serving, and the rest of the game is open.

Despite these similarities and differences, athletes across the spectrum are often internally distracted by the qualities of their opponents and are sizing up whether or not they are going to be successful, in part based on how they view their opponents.

One of the things I try to guide athletes toward is an awareness that they are only in control of themselves and that the opponent they would be wise to try to "beat" is themselves.

"Can you be a little more disciplined?"

"Can you be a little more intentional?"

"Can you push a little more in this drill?"

Putting an emphasis on what you can control and challenging yourself to be your best minimizes the internal distraction that can flow from the interference that accompanies too much thinking about your opponent.

As the former tennis legend Arthur Ashe once said, "You are never really playing an opponent. You are playing yourself, your own highest standards, and when you reach your limits, that is real joy."

143

THE GAME CARES **WHAT YOU DO,** NOT HOW YOU FEEL

AS THE "EMOTIONS-AND-FEELINGS GUY" IN SO MANY SPORTS organizations over the years, I am called upon daily to assist athletes and coaches in the management and regulation of their feelings. One of the phrases I use surprises some of my clients the first time they hear it. I tell them, "The game cares about what you do, not how you feel."

This is not a departure from being sensitive to and aware of the importance of emotional control. Instead, this is my way of reminding the athlete that no matter how they feel, it is their actions that will ultimately determine the quality of their performance.

Many athletes give too much weight and power to their emotions in situations where action is required. Not feeling confident, feeling unmotivated, or feeling scared or nervous does not necessarily mean that the actions or the execution of a skill is going to be compromised. Certainly, sometimes these emotions can influence the quality of our execution, but there are any number of times where an athlete won't exactly "feel right" and they still execute well enough to compete and potentially win. I hear every day about athletes who felt "off" and still won competitions big and small.

My advice? Recognize if you're stressing about being stressed or scared because you're scared. Remind yourself about the multiple times where you haven't felt perfect but still performed or trained quite adequately. **Behave, act, and execute to the best of your ability, no matter how you feel emotionally, and do not let your feelings be an excuse or a reason for not giving 100 percent effort.**

Sometimes you will not have the time or the technique or the awareness to fully manage your emotions into a "perfect" place. The game doesn't know this, nor does your opponent. It's up to you to act with boldness to the degree you can muster it and let your actions speak louder than your feelings.

144

IF YOU PUT IN X

AS A BELIEVER IN MANY OF THE TEACHINGS OF THE GREAT psychologist Albert Ellis, I work to educate athletes about his theory regarding irrational beliefs.

An example of this is when athletes get internally sidetracked, discouraged, or upset by the fact that things don't turn out in the ways that they think they "should":

> "I worked so hard at developing that skill—I should have played better."
> "I really sacrificed a lot for this opportunity, so I should have been on the podium."
> "I know I work harder than that athlete—there's no way they should have beaten me."

When I hear these types of statements from athletes, I remind them that it is nonsensical or irrational to think that just because they put a certain amount of energy into something, they are now guaranteed anything. Unfortunately, far too many athletes who are unsuccessful after having gone through a tough stretch of training or preparation go on to become discouraged or disillusioned or distrustful of their training process. While it is wise to reconsider what worked and what didn't work in the training process in order to refine one's preparation, oftentimes athletes take an extreme view and feel as though their work entitled them to a certain outcome. Then they become extremely distressed when that outcome doesn't occur. They proceed to abandon their training method or work less diligently or allow the momentary setback to negatively influence their motivation or belief. All of these responses are unhelpful and might negatively affect the athlete's next training block or competition.

The fact that you put in a certain amount of energy, work, or effort only increases the likelihood that you have earned an increased chance at the success you seek. Keep in mind that there are any number of factors that contribute to your achieving the goals you seek. Don't delude yourself into thinking that the work you put in ensures anything. Just know that what you're doing is making success more likely, and strive to be at peace with that.

145

MONITOR YOUR **ENERGY EXPENDITURE**

AMONG THE HOT TOPICS IN THE WORLD TODAY IS THE ISSUE OF climate change. Regardless of what one's view of the world is or what one believes philosophically, there is little denying that our climate is experiencing some radical extremes. This challenge is being met by a multitude of approaches and opinions around "how we got here" and "what we can do about it."

Similarly, as an athlete, your internal climate is prone to extremes. There are times when you burn "too hot" and times when you are not engaged enough, aware enough, or energized enough. When that happens, the first thing to do is to increase your self-awareness about what your internal climate is like and be aware of how you get feedback when you're running "too hot" or "too cold."

This entails identifying your observation mechanism, which might be something like:

My feet have stopped moving.
I'm losing composure.
I'm becoming impulsive.

This allows you the opportunity to adjust your energy. Many athletes burn excessive energy pre-training or pre-performance through an overactivation of thoughts of worry, fear, or stress:

This is going to be a hard workout.
I'm not sure how I'm going to play today.
My competition looks really fit.
Coach looks like she's in a really bad mood.

Thoughts like these then lead to unnecessary "fuel" being burned that has nothing to do with eliciting great performance. Similarly, in the midst of training or in the middle of a competition, **you have an obligation to yourself to implement strategies that will moderate your internal "temperature" so you can minimize the likelihood of going to an "extreme."**

Just as the world's leaders cannot agree on the specific implementation strategies that are best for their constituency, it is difficult for many athletes to choose specific strategies that will be effective for them. Instead, many athletes do nothing and just "hope" it takes care of itself.

"Once I make a couple of baskets."
"Once I get a hit."
"Once I score a goal."

They are waiting for some outcome to influence their internal environment. I would urge you as an athlete, just as I would urge our world's leaders, to work on effecting *any strategy* that has potential so you can at least gather information about its effectiveness. To choose to do nothing to purposefully adjust and regulate your internal energy "burn" is like taking your hands off the steering wheel when driving a car and hoping it all turns out well. Take control of your self-regulation through awareness and decisive action of some kind and then implement a feedback loop to help you assess how well your strategy works for future use or adjustment.

146

APPRECIATE **THE SUCCESS** OF OTHERS

AN EXTREMELY COMPETITIVE WORLD AND THE EXTREMELY competitive culture of athletics tends to feed a "dog-eat-dog" mindset, leaving little room to appreciate or give a nod to the successes of others. We've all heard things like:

> "It's either you or them."
> "If you're not getting better, your competition will catch you."

Thoughts like this and cultures built around this sort of paradigm view nearly everything as a zero-sum game:

> "If I win, you necessarily must lose."
> "Every gain you make takes away something from me."

Seeing things in this way is particularly toxic in a team environment.

Mental performance coach Brett Ledbetter does a nice job of describing this in one of his *What Drives Winning* videos. He makes an important distinction between competing *against* your teammates versus competing *with* your teammates. Competing against sets up the mindset that *I don't want you to succeed too much because it might take away my playing time, my opportunity to make varsity, my chances of getting selected for the traveling team, my odds of getting the promotion, or whatever.* In this way, it feels like every time my teammate does well, it potentially takes something away from me. While at times this might be objectively true, quite often the side effect of this is team members not wishing one another well, even secretly hoping they don't do well, which breaks down bonds and chemistry within a team.

With a notion of competing *with* your teammates, it's possible to recognize that oftentimes sport is not a zero-sum game. *I can get better, and so can you. You getting better can push me to get better, and we both improve on our own pathway toward mastery. Ultimately, this helps the team win.*

In many of the teams I've worked with that have won international medals, world championships, or national championships, there is an internal battle within the team where each team member is taking advantage of a culture of hard work, pursuing excellence, and competing with or alongside someone who is doggedly determined to improve each day. This does not have to become rivalry. This does not have to trigger envy or jealousy. It can, instead, stimulate and activate the athlete to push themselves above and beyond what they might believe possible. This sort of mindset increases the likelihood that each individual maximizes their contribution to the team's ultimate success.

147

GAP VS. FOUNDATION

IT'S A CHALLENGE FOR MOST ATHLETES TO REMEMBER HOW good they are. While I never want any athlete to have an overinflated sense of themselves, I absolutely want them to keep in mind what they bring to their athletic environment every day—essentially, the sum total of their preparation, training, and competition experience from the first day they began their journey as an athlete.

One of the reasons why many athletes are challenged to remember how good they are is that they are often mesmerized by how good they want to be or what it would be like to make it to the next level in their sport. Aspiring to be an improved version of themselves is what I would want for every athlete. However, if that aspiration becomes a fixation on the gap between where they currently are and where they want to be, it can sometimes fracture the foundation upon which they stand.

I often quantify this in generic terms when describing this phenomenon to an athlete: "Let's say the best athlete in the world in your sport is quantifiably 100. Let's say that currently, you are about an 80—however we define it. If you get too worried about or obsessed with the 20 points you have not yet amassed as an athlete, you can lose sight of the 80 you are standing on foundationally. **The desire to**

be at the next level, to move toward mastery, to grow and develop as an athlete, is the fuel that drives you to work hard and expand your skills intentionally. I always want you to remember the 80 you are as you strive for the next 20 you are not yet."

In being critical about their deficits, a lot of athletes fail to remember the skills and tools they fundamentally possess or have available to them. I want them to consistently be reminded about their foundation and not be overly distracted by the gap they want to close in their future.

The most mentally disciplined athletes remain aware of the foundational traits they possess. Those with lesser discipline are constantly reacting to the wavering state they are in:

"I feel great today."
"I feel like I can't get it right today."
"I feel like I've lost it."
"I feel like it's easy."

The "traits vs. state" notion has huge implications. Maintaining awareness of your permanent foundational traits is key to stable and sustained confidence. Attention given to the fluctuating momentary state that you are in puts your confidence on a rollercoaster ride.

Do you give more power to the years of foundational work or how you "feel" in a fleeting moment?

148

HOW WOULD IT BE TO **FACE YOU?**

COMMONLY, ATHLETES HAVE A TENDENCY TO SIZE UP THEIR prospective opponents before they compete. Constructively, this can be used to develop strategies, game plans, and tactics in order to be able to devise plans to ultimately give the athlete a chance to win.

As well, what sometimes occurs is that the athlete becomes anxious about their opponent because they see their opponent as "too good," "so fast," or "so skilled." There can often be nonproductive concerns generated in an athlete's mind because of what they perceive to be the high quality of their opponent.

One of the ways I deal with this with the athletes with whom I work is to remind them, "Your opponent has to deal with you." As a regular exercise, I like to ask the athlete in front of me to speak about the strengths and the qualities that make them a successful athlete. We identify the tools in their proverbial toolbox, and I guide them to speak to the challenges that their opponent encounters when facing them. I will not denigrate or speak down about an opponent's potential skill set. However, **I want to constantly remind athletes of the qualities *they* possess that their opponent has to try to handle.**

Having an athlete write a scouting report about themselves, with an appreciation and understanding of how difficult it will be for someone to overcome all of their assets, can both increase the confidence of the athlete and also help them recognize it is going to be challenging for their opponent to face them. In reality, the reverse may also be true—the opponent may be thinking about how good the athlete I am working with is, and they might be anxious to face them.

In the end, I really don't want my client focusing too much on what's going on in their opponent's head. However, I do want them to take a moment to understand that they present a challenge for any opponent to overcome and that they would do well to understand and remember that someone else having to deal with their skill set would be a tough duty as well.

149

FORGET A BALANCED LIFE

IN MY EXPERIENCE, THE VAST MAJORITY OF PEOPLE ARE unwilling to do what it takes to be among the elite, in part because they are unwilling to make the investments and sacrifices necessary to give themselves their ultimate chance. As stated elsewhere, I have no judgment on this. I am among the majority disinclined to go "all in," and I made that choice intentionally and deliberately. I have consciously chosen a more balanced life over being exceptional at any one particular thing.

On the other hand, for those very few who are actually willing to do "whatever it takes," what comes along with that is the reality that their lives, while they are engaged in their pursuit of excellence, are going to be unbalanced relative to the norm.

Former NBA star Kobe Bryant put it this way: "Throw out the idea of a 'balanced' life if you want to be great. Some people try to balance their love with other interests, but there is no such thing as balance, my man. Either you want to be one of the greats, and you understand the sacrifices that come with it and deal with them, or you don't want to deal with them and you end up in the middle of the pack."

I would argue that for **those willing to live the unbalanced life in pursuit of mastery, they might suffer unintended consequences—**

relationally, financially, physically, or mentally/emotionally. Certainly, I have encountered my fair percentage of "all-in" athletes who have suffered loss or deprivation in another area of their lives. However, for those who have risen to the pinnacle of their profession—and I've been around a lot of them as well—the sacrifices and investments made were a part of the reason why they were as successful in their craft as they were. They were willing to live with any ramification or consequence along the way.

For most, there may be a willingness to engage in that "unbalanced" lifestyle for a short period of time. Maybe it's a collegiate athlete willing to go "all in" for their four years of college. Maybe it's a triathlete who is willing to make sacrifices for *x* number of years in order to see how far that takes them in their training and races.

The point is that to try to live a balanced life and do what is necessary to be among the elite is a nearly impossible task. On the other hand, knowing that choosing the unbalanced lifestyle—even temporarily—is likely to create some life challenges outside of your pursuits is valuable information that can be used to make more informed decisions about the potential implications of your choices.

150

SQUEEZE OUT THE **LAST DROPS**

WHEN AN ATHLETE REACHES THE END OF THEIR COMPETITION, the end of their season, or the end of their career, I often hear them lament something significant they had influence over:

> "I could have been more courageous as a competitor."
> "I wish I had taken more acceptable risks."
> "I feel like I contaminated the enjoyment of my final season."
> "I would have liked to have been more willing to be aggressive rather than defaulting to tentative when the stakes were high."

In a micro sense, embracing courageous action and enhancing gratitude can help one fight through challenging moments in a training session or a contest. In a macro sense, this same notion applies as one tries to "squeeze every last drop" out of their season or career.

Getting the absolute most out of the end of one's season or career is something that is important for athletes to proactively address:

> "How can I get great closure?"
> "How can I take advantage of the time that remains?"

> "When I look back on this experience, what will I want to have done, fulfilled, or emphasized?"

Getting adequate closure on a contest, a season, or a career can be very rewarding. It allows you to walk away from the situation gracefully, feeling some sense of satisfaction—independent of the results.

As with many things related to mental skill development in life and in sport, it is as simple and as difficult as that. Choose your mindset and align it with behaviors that reflect that mindset. Ultimately, **if you can finish your season or career knowing you competed in a way that aligned with your values—whether that be courage, humility, a team-first attitude, etc.—you can be accepting of any outcome.**

A FINAL WORD ON TRUST AND COMMITMENT

I have previously explained the importance of distinguishing between *commitment* and *trust*. This has application in the precise moment of executing your task with assertiveness—independent of deep belief or trust that it will turn out okay. In another entry we spoke about the benefit of committing to a coach's input in order to potentially fully trust it and also the benefit of the coach fully committing to the athlete in order to give the athlete the latitude to earn the coach's trust. **This last application speaks to the long-term, big-picture impact of having enough *commitment* to a long-standing process so that you can eventually build *trust* in its efficacy.**

I use this story to distinguish the difference between commitment and trust in a long-term sense. Nearly four decades ago, when I proposed to my wife, I did not trust the institution of marriage. Both of my parents had been married three times, and I had no clear role models for establishing healthy, long-lasting relationships. Still, at that time, I chose to make a strong, concrete commitment to my fiancée. I committed to the daily actions of being as good of a husband as I could be. I took courageous action, and over time my daily commitment developed into a deep trust in the marriage that thrives to this day. Had I waited to trust marriage before I was willing to commit, I may still be waiting.

In the utilization of some of the concepts in this book, let's explore a couple of pointed questions:

1. Do you trust that making intentional adjustments based on what you've learned in here will work out well for you?
   It doesn't matter, as long as you're willing to commit to making the committed effort intentionally and long enough to see if you can trust the method or change.
2. Do you trust that if you put in the effort, your life is going to turn out as you'd like?
   We don't get to know how anything turns out until the end.

One challenge facing many of us is the same one facing some coaches as they guide and develop athletes. A lot of people undershoot their potential because either they don't believe it's possible to get to the next level—they don't see themselves as good enough—or they are waiting for some sort of "guarantee" so that they can trust it will work out before they put in the work. I suggest that you reframe this in the context of commitment: Don't worry about if or when you are going to get to that level. Don't fret about whether you trust that it's going to work out in the long term or not. Don't let that be a distraction. Go tackle today's tasks with full commitment and courage, and give yourself the best chance to live the life experiences of your dreams.

APPENDIX: WHAT'S HOLDING YOU BACK?

Score yourself on a scale of 1–10 where 1 means "Absolutely not a challenge for me" and 10 means "A very difficult challenge for me." There is no right or wrong response. A score of 7 or higher indicates the topic merits attention.

___ Comparing myself to others
___ Being consumed by results
___ Getting over mistakes
___ Dealing with expectations from others
___ Confronting people
___ Knowing who am I outside of sport (or without it)
___ Fearing failure
___ Lacking motivation
___ Listening to the wrong (negative) voice in my head
___ Dealing with pressure
___ Playing free
___ Having the inability to ever please myself (I'm never happy with my accomplishments)
___ Understanding my purpose for playing
___ Dealing with outside criticism
___ Possessing self-doubts (having a lack of confidence)
___ Caring too much about recognition and status (upholding my reputation)
___ Having realistic expectations of myself

___ Understanding that team success is more important than my individual success

___ Demonstrating emotional control (with frustration, anger, etc.)

___ Tying my self-worth to my performance

___ Developing good interpersonal relationships (with coaches, teammates, peers, etc.)

___ Having good time-management skills (including being able to prioritize)

___ Caring too much about what others think about me

___ Dealing with controlling parents

___ Keeping my love for the game

___ Accepting constructive criticism from teammates and coaches

___ Giving constructive criticism to teammates

___ Resisting the urge to be perfect

___ Being able to adapt in a new environment

___ Dealing with loneliness

___ Fearing success

___ Dealing with judgment (from myself and others)

___ Judging other people

___ Having a solid work ethic

___ Seeking validation from others

___ Struggling with trusting others

___ Dealing with not being accepted

___ Leaving my comfort zone

___ Losing perspective of all the great opportunities sport brings me

___ Making excuses (not going "all in")

___ Accepting my role

___ Having the discipline to stick to a plan

___ Keeping my personal problems away from my sport environment

REFERENCES

Brown, Brené. *Dare to Lead: Brave Work. Tough Conversations.* Whole Hearts. New York: Random House, 2018.

Clarey, Christopher. *The Master: The Long Run and Beautiful Game of Roger Federer.* New York: Twelve, 2021.

Clear, James. *Atomic Habits: An Easy and Proven Way to Build Good Habits and Break Bad Ones.* New York: Avery, 2018.

Elmore, Tim. Growing Leaders curriculum, "Habitudes for Athletes." Growing Leaders, powered by Maxwell Leadership Foundation, www.growingleaders.com/curriculum/.

Harvey, Joan, Ph.D., with Cynthia Katz. *If I'm So Successful, Why Do I Feel Like a Fake?: The Impostor Phenomenon.* New York: St. Martin's Press, 1985.

Keen, Sam. *Fire in the Belly: On Being a Man.* New York: Bantam, 1992.

Kross, Ethan. *Chatter: The Voice in Our Head, Why It Matters, and How to Harness It.* New York: Crown, 2021.

Ledbetter, Brett. "How to Stop Comparing and Start Competing." TEDx Gateway Arch, YouTube, uploaded by TEDx Talks, 26 January 2017, https://www.youtube.com/watch?v=bU09Y9sC7JY.

Moawad, Trevor. *It Takes What It Takes: How to Think Neutrally and Gain Control of Your Life.* New York: HarperOne, 2020.

Sapolsky, Robert. *Why Zebras Don't Get Ulcers: The Acclaimed Guide to Stress, Stress-Related Diseases, and Coping*, Third Edition. New York: Holt, 2004.

Syed, Matthew. *Black Box Thinking: Why Most People Never Learn from Their Mistakes—But Some Do.* New York: Portfolio, 2015.

ACKNOWLEDGMENTS

First and foremost, I want to acknowledge Renee Jardine, the editor of this book. There is zero chance that this book would have been written were it not for her constant encouragement, professional wisdom and guidance, and patience with my neurotic idiosyncrasies, which had me questioning and feeling insecure about this process through its entirety. Thank you so much, Renee, for your kindness, your unflappability, and your hand-holding throughout this project.

My deepest gratitude to my friends and family members who have supported my professional journey and granted unwavering love and regard for me and my career path.

This began with a passion for sport that was instilled in me at a very young age.

Thank you for the love and encouragement and support that sustained me through many difficult times in my personal and professional journey. Thank you for the backing at home that I have received 100 percent of the time—without complaint—as my work often had me working seven days a week and flying all over the country. Thank you to my closest circle for the cheerleading and unconditional love that I have received and continue to receive when things have felt shaky. Knowing that you are always there for me is the bedrock upon which I stand, and my life's greatest blessing.

ABOUT THE AUTHOR

JEFF TROESCH is a mental performance specialist with a storied career spent working alongside professional, elite amateur, and collegiate athletes and coaches.

An internationally renowned expert in mental skills training and performance enhancement with nearly 40 years of experience, Troesch began his career as a consultant with the NBA. From there, he went on to assist the Seattle Mariners and Detroit Tigers in Major League Baseball, the US Soccer Federation, USA Track & Field, IMG Academy in Bradenton, Florida, and numerous touring golf and tennis pros. He also consulted in the development of the VS training system, a mobile brain-training device that was piloted in several major sports organizations, including teams in the NBA, MLB, and the NFL.

At the collegiate level, Troesch has played an integral role in developing student-athletes at dozens of major universities, including UCLA, UC Berkeley, Stanford, and Cal Poly. His contribution is wide-ranging and includes input into team building, ongoing team consultation, and individual athlete consultation regarding mental conditioning and performance enhancement, as well as coach consulting and development.

Troesch is also accomplished in cultivating talent in individual sports, particularly tennis, golf, track and field, and endurance sports. He oversaw a staff of mental trainers as Director of Sports Psychology for IMG Academy in Florida, where he was instrumental in the development of their mental conditioning program, after which eleven of his former clients rose to be ranked No. 1 in the world in either singles or doubles. As Director of Mental Training for David Leadbetter's Golf Academies worldwide, Troesch helped to shape the development of the training programs and methodology that continues to produce golf champions around the world. Among his golf clients' successes are wins on professional tours all over the globe. He has worked with multiple NCAA individual and team champions, was the mental consultant for the US Solheim Cup team in 2022, and has guided multiple winners of the US Amateur and US Women's Amateur Championships.

His clients have won dozens of medals at world championships and Olympic Games in a broad number of sports since 1988.

Jeff Troesch lives in and consults out of San Luis Obispo, California.